# Practical Data Wrangling

Expert techniques for transforming your raw data into a
valuable source for analytics

**Allan Visochek**

BIRMINGHAM - MUMBAI

# Practical Data Wrangling

First published: November 2017

Production reference: 1141117

Published by Packt Publishing Ltd.
Livery Place
35 Livery Street
Birmingham
B3 2PB, UK.

ISBN 978-1-78728-613-9

www.packtpub.com

# Credits

**Author**
Allan Visochek

**Reviewer**
Adriano Longo

**Commissioning Editor**
Amey Varangaonkar

**Acquisition Editor**
Malaika Monteiro

**Content Development Editor**
Aaryaman Singh

**Technical Editor**
Dinesh Chaudhary

**Copy Editors**
Tasneem Fatehi
Safis Editing

**Project Coordinator**
Manthan Patel

**Proofreader**
Safis Editing

**Indexer**
Pratik Shirodkar

**Graphics**
Tania Dutta

**Production Coordinator**
Shraddha Falebhai

# About the Author

**Allan Visochek** is a freelance web developer and data analyst in New Haven, Connecticut. Outside of work, Allan has a deep interest in machine learning and artificial intelligence.

Allan thoroughly enjoys teaching and sharing knowledge. After graduating from the Udacity Data Analyst Nanodegree program, he was contracted to Udacity for several months as a forum mentor and project reviewer, offering guidance to students working on data analysis projects. He has also written technical content for learntoprogram.tv.

# About the Reviewer

**Adriano Longo** is a freelance data analyst based in the Netherlands with a passion for Neo4j's relationship-oriented data model.

He specializes in querying, processing, and modeling data with Cypher, R, Python, and SQL, and worked on climate prediction models at UEA's Climatic Research Unit before focusing on analytical solutions for the private sector.

Today, Adriano uses Neo4j and linkurious.js to explore the complex web of relationships nefarious actors use to obfuscate their abuse of environmental and financial regulations, making dirty secrets less transparent, one graph at a time.

# www.PacktPub.com

For support files and downloads related to your book, please visit www.PacktPub.com. Did you know that Packt offers eBook versions of every book published, with PDF and ePub files available? You can upgrade to the eBook version at www.PacktPub.com and as a print book customer, you are entitled to a discount on the eBook copy. Get in touch with us at service@packtpub.com for more details. At www.PacktPub.com, you can also read a collection of free technical articles, sign up for a range of free newsletters and receive exclusive discounts and offers on Packt books and eBooks.

https://www.packtpub.com/mapt

Get the most in-demand software skills with Mapt. Mapt gives you full access to all Packt books and video courses, as well as industry-leading tools to help you plan your personal development and advance your career.

# Why subscribe?

- Fully searchable across every book published by Packt
- Copy and paste, print, and bookmark content
- On demand and accessible via a web browser

# Customer Feedback

Thanks for purchasing this Packt book. At Packt, quality is at the heart of our editorial process. To help us improve, please leave us an honest review on this book's Amazon page at `https://www.amazon.com/dp/1787286134`. If you'd like to join our team of regular reviewers, you can email us at `customerreviews@packtpub.com`. We award our regular reviewers with free eBooks and videos in exchange for their valuable feedback. Help us be relentless in improving our products!

# Table of Contents

# Preface

Data rarely comes prepared for its end use. For any particular project, there may be too much data, too little data, missing data, erroneous data, poorly structured data, or improperly formatted data. This book is about how to gather the data that is available and produce an output that is ready to be used. In each of the chapters, one or more demonstrations are used to show a new approach to data wrangling.

# What this book covers

Chapter 1, *Programming with Data*, discusses the context of data wrangling and offers a high-level overview of the rest of the book's content.

**Section 1: A generalized programming approach to data wrangling**

Chapter 2, *Introduction to Programming in Python*, introduces programming using the Python programming language, which used in most of the chapters of the book.

Chapter 3, *Reading, Exploring, and Modifying Data - Part I*, is an overview of the steps for processing a data file and an introduction to JSON data.

Chapter 4, *Reading, Exploring, and Modifying Data - Part II*, continues from the previous chapter, extending to the CSV and XML data formats.

Chapter 5, *Manipulating Text Data - An Introduction to Regular Expressions*, is an introduction to regular expressions with the application of extracting street names from street addresses.

**Section 2: A formulated approach to data wrangling**

Chapter 6, *Cleaning Numerical Data - An Introduction to R and RStudio*, introduces R and RStudio with the application of cleaning numerical data.

Chapter 7, *Simplifying Data Manipulation with dplyr*, is an introduction to the dplyr package for R, which can be used to express multiple data processing steps elegantly and concisely.

**Section 3: Advanced methods for retrieving and storing data**

Chapter 8, *Getting Data from the Web*, is an introduction to APIs. This chapter shows how to extract data from APIs using Python.

Chapter 9, *Working with Large Datasets*, has an overview of the issues when working with large amounts of data and a very brief introduction to MongoDB.

# What you need for this book

You will need a Python 3 installation on your computer, and you will need to be able to execute Python from your operating system's command-line interface. In addition, the following external Python modules will be used:

- pandas (Chapters 4 and 5)
- requests (Chapter 8)
- PyMongo (Chapter 9)

For Chapter 9, you will need to install MongoDB and set up your own local MongoDB server.
For Chapters 6 and 7, you will need RStudio and Rbase. Additionally, for Chapter 7, you will need the dplyr and tibble libraries.

# Who this book is for

If you are a data scientist, data analyst, or statistician who wants to learn how to wrangle your data for analysis in the best possible manner, this book is for you. As this book covers both R and Python, some understanding of these will be beneficial.

# Conventions

In this book, you will find a number of text styles that distinguish between different kinds of information. Here are some examples of these styles and an explanation of their meaning.

Code words in text, database table names, folder names, filenames, file extensions, pathnames, dummy URLs, user input, and Twitter handles are shown as follows: "The next lines of code read the link and assign it to the open function."

A block of code is set as follows:

```
fin = open('data/fake_weather_data.csv','r',newline='')
reader = csv.reader(fin)
for row in reader:
    myData.append(row)
```

When we wish to draw your attention to a particular part of a code block, the relevant lines or items are set in bold:

```
new_scf_data = []
for old_entry in scf_data["issues"]:
    new_entry={}
```

Any command-line input or output is written as follows:

```
$ mongoimport --file fake_weather_data.csv
```

**New terms** and **important words** are shown in bold.

Words that you see on the screen, for example, in menus or dialog boxes, appear in the text like this: "In order to download new modules, we will go to **Files** | **Settings** | **Project Name** | **Project Interpreter**."

Warnings or important notes appear like this.

Tips and tricks appear like this.

# Reader feedback

Feedback from our readers is always welcome. Let us know what you think about this book-what you liked or disliked. Reader feedback is important for us as it helps us develop titles that you will really get the most out of. To send us general feedback, simply email feedback@packtpub.com, and mention the book's title in the subject of your message. If there is a topic that you have expertise in and you are interested in either writing or contributing to a book, see our author guide at www.packtpub.com/authors.

# Customer support

Now that you are the proud owner of a Packt book, we have a number of things to help you to get the most from your purchase.

# Downloading the example code

You can download the example code files for this book from your account at `http://www.packtpub.com`. If you purchased this book elsewhere, you can visit `http://www.packtpub.com/support` and register to have the files emailed directly to you. You can download the code files by following these steps:

1. Log in or register to our website using your email address and password.
2. Hover the mouse pointer on the **SUPPORT** tab at the top.
3. Click on **Code Downloads & Errata**.
4. Enter the name of the book in the **Search** box.
5. Select the book for which you're looking to download the code files.
6. Choose from the drop-down menu where you purchased this book from.
7. Click on **Code Download**.

Once the file is downloaded, please make sure that you unzip or extract the folder using the latest version of:

- WinRAR / 7-Zip for Windows
- Zipeg / iZip / UnRarX for Mac
- 7-Zip / PeaZip for Linux

The code bundle for the book is also hosted on GitHub at `https://github.com/PacktPublishing/Practical-Data-Wrangling`. We also have other code bundles from our rich catalog of books and videos available at `https://github.com/PacktPublishing/`. Check them out!

# Downloading the color images of this book

We also provide you with a PDF file that has color images of the screenshots/diagrams used in this book. The color images will help you better understand the changes in the output. You can download this file from `https://www.packtpub.com/sites/default/files/downloads/PracticalDataWrangling_ColorImages.pdf`.

# Errata

Although we have taken every care to ensure the accuracy of our content, mistakes do happen. If you find a mistake in one of our books-maybe a mistake in the text or the code- we would be grateful if you could report this to us. By doing so, you can save other readers from frustration and help us improve subsequent versions of this book. If you find any errata, please report them by visiting http://www.packtpub.com/submit-errata, selecting your book, clicking on the **Errata Submission Form** link, and entering the details of your errata. Once your errata are verified, your submission will be accepted and the errata will be uploaded to our website or added to any list of existing errata under the Errata section of that title. To view the previously submitted errata, go to https://www.packtpub.com/books/content/support and enter the name of the book in the search field. The required information will appear under the **Errata** section.

# Piracy

Piracy of copyrighted material on the internet is an ongoing problem across all media. At Packt, we take the protection of our copyright and licenses very seriously. If you come across any illegal copies of our works in any form on the internet, please provide us with the location address or website name immediately so that we can pursue a remedy. Please contact us at copyright@packtpub.com with a link to the suspected pirated material. We appreciate your help in protecting our authors and our ability to bring you valuable content.

# Questions

If you have a problem with any aspect of this book, you can contact us at questions@packtpub.com, and we will do our best to address the problem.

# 1
# Programming with Data

It takes a lot of time and effort to deliver data in a format that is ready for its end use. Let's use an example of an online gaming site that wants to post the high score for each of its games every month. In order to make this data available, the site's developers would need to set up a database to keep data on all of the scores. In addition, they would need a system to retrieve the top scores every month from that database and display it to the end users.

For the users of our hypothetical gaming site, getting this month's high scores is fairly straightforward. This is because finding out what the high scores are is a rather general use case. A lot of people will want that specific data in that specific form, so it makes sense to develop a system to deliver the monthly high scores.

Unlike the users of our hypothetical gaming site, data programmers have very specialized use cases for the data that they work with. A data journalist following politics may want to visualize trends in government spending over the last few years. A machine learning engineer working in the medical industry may want to develop an algorithm to predict a patient's likelihood of returning to the hospital after a visit. A statistician working for the board of education may want to investigate the correlation between attendance and test scores. In the gaming site example, a data analyst may want to investigate how the distribution of scores changes based on the time of the day.

**A short side note on terminology**:
**Data science** as an all encompassing term can be a bit elusive. As it is such a new field, the definition of a data scientist can change depending on who you ask. To be more general, the term **data programmer** will be used in this book to refer to anyone who will find data wrangling useful in their work.

Drawing insight from data requires that all the information that is needed is in a format that you can work with. Organizations that produce data (for example, governments, schools, hospitals, and web applications) can't anticipate the exact information that any given data programmer might need for their work. There are too many possible scenarios to make it worthwhile. Data is therefore generally made available in its raw format. Sometimes this is enough to work with, but usually it is not. Here are some common reasons:

- There may be extra steps involved in getting the data
- The information needed may be spread across multiple sources
- Datasets may be too large to work with in their original format
- There may be far more fields or information in a particular dataset than needed
- Datasets may have misspellings, missing fields, mixed formats, incorrect entries, outliers, and so on
- Datasets may be structured or formatted in a way that is not compatible with a particular application

Due to this, it is often the responsibility of the data programmer to perform the following functions:

- Discover and gather the data that is needed (getting data)
- Merge data from different sources if necessary (merging data)
- Fix flaws in the data entries (cleaning data)
- Extract the necessary data and put it in the proper structure (shaping data)
- Store it in the proper format for further use (storing data)

This perspective helps give some context to the relevance and importance of data wrangling. Data wrangling is sometimes seen as the grunt work of the data programmer, but it is nevertheless an integral part of drawing insights from data. This book will guide you through the various skill sets, most common tools, and best practices for data wrangling. In the following section, I will break down the tasks involved in data wrangling and provide a broad overview of the rest of the book. I will discuss the following steps in detail and provide some examples:

- Getting data
- Cleaning data
- Merging and shaping data
- Storing data

Following the high-level overview, I will briefly discuss Python and R, the tools used in this book to conduct data wrangling.

# Understanding data wrangling

**Data wrangling**, broadly speaking, is the process of gathering data in its raw form and molding it into a form that is suitable for its end use. Preparing data for its end use can branch out into a number of different tasks based on the exact use case. This can make it rather hard to pin down exactly what data wrangling entails, and formulate how to go about it. Nevertheless, there are a number of common steps in the data wrangling process, as outlined in the following subsections. The approach that I will take in this book is to introduce a number of tools and practices that are often involved in data wrangling. Each of the chapters will consist of one or more exercises and/or projects that will demonstrate the application of a particular tool or approach.

# Getting and reading data

The first step is to retrieve a dataset and open it with a program capable of manipulating the data. The simplest way of retrieving a dataset is to find a data file. *Python* and *R* can be used to open, read, modify, and save data stored in static files. In Chapter 3, *Reading, Exploring, and Modifying Data - Part I*, I will introduce the JSON data format and show how to use Python to read, write and modify JSON data. In Chapter 4, *Reading, Exploring, and Modifying Data - Part II*, I will walk through how to use Python to work with data files in the CSV and XML data formats. In Chapter 6, *Cleaning Numerical Data - An Introduction to R and Rstudio*, I will introduce R and Rstudio, and show how to use R to read and manipulate data.

Larger data sources are often made available through web interfaces called **application programming interfaces** (**APIs**). APIs allow you to retrieve specific bits of data from a larger collection of data. Web APIs can be great resources for data that is otherwise hard to get. In Chapter 8, *Getting Data from the Web*, I discuss APIs in detail and walk through the use of Python to extract data from APIs.

Another possible source of data is a **database.** I won't go into detail on the use of databases in this book, though in Chapter 9, *Working with Large Datasets*, I will show how to interact with a particular database using Python.

**Databases** are collections of data that are organized to optimize the quick retrieval of data. They can be particularly useful when we need to work incrementally on very large datasets, and of course may be a source of data.

# Cleaning data

When working with data, you can generally expect to find human errors, missing entries, and numerical outliers. These types of errors usually need to be corrected, handled, or removed to prepare a dataset for analysis.

In Chapter 5, *Manipulating Text Data - An Introduction to Regular Expressions*, I will demonstrate how to use **regular expressions**, a tool to identify, extract, and modify patterns in text data. Chapter 5, *Manipulating Text Data - An Introduction to Regular Expressions*, includes a project to use regular expressions to extract street names.

In Chapter 6, *Cleaning Numerical Data - An Introduction to R and Rstudio*, I will demonstrate how to use RStudio to conduct two common tasks for cleaning numerical data: outlier detection and NA handling.

# Shaping and structuring data

Preparing data for its end use often requires both structuring and organizing the data in the correct manner.

To illustrate this, suppose you have a hierarchical dataset of city populations, as shown in *Figure 01:*

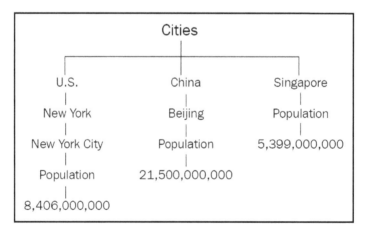

Figure 01: Hierarchical structure of the population of cities

If the goal is to create a histogram of city populations, the previous data format would be hard to work with. Not only is the information of the city populations nested within the data structure, but it is nested to varying degrees of depth. For the purposes of creating a histogram, it is better to represent the data as a list of numbers, as shown in *Figure 02*:

[ 8406000000 , 21500000000 , 5399000000 ]

Figure 02: List of populations for histogram visualization

Making structural changes like this for large datasets requires you to build programs that can extract the data from one format and put it into another format. Shaping data is an important part of data wrangling because it ensures that the data is compatible with its intended use. In Chapter 4, *Reading, Exploring, and Modifying Data - Part II*, I will walk through exercises to convert between data formats.

Changing the form of data does not necessarily need to involve changing its structure. Changing the form of a dataset can involve filtering the data entries, reducing the data by category, changing the order of the rows, and changing the way columns are set up.

All of the previously mentioned tasks are features of the dplyr package for R. In Chapter 7, *Simplifying Data Manipulation with dplyr*, I will show how to use dplyr to easily and intuitively manipulate data.

# Storing data

The last step after manipulating a dataset is to store the data for future use. The easiest way to do this is to store the data in a static file. I show how to output the data to a static file in Python in Chapters 3, *Reading, Exploring, and Modifying Data - Part I* and Chapter 4, *Reading, Analyzing, Modifying, and Writing Data - Part II*. I show how to do this in R in Chapter 6, *Cleaning Numerical Data - An Introduction to R and Rstudio*.

When working with large datasets, it can be helpful to have a system that allows you to store and quickly retrieve large amounts of data when needed.

In addition to being a potential source of data, databases can be very useful in the process of data wrangling as a means of storing data locally. In Chapter 9, *Working with Large Datasets*, I will briefly demonstrate the use of databases to store data.

# The tools for data wrangling

The most popular languages used for data wrangling are Python and R. I will use the remaining part of this chapter to introduce Python and R, and briefly discuss the differences between them.

# Python

**Python** is a generalized programming language used for everything from web development (Django and Flask) to game development, and for scientific and numerical computation. See `Python.org/about/apps/`.

Python is really useful for data wrangling and scientific computing in general because it emphasizes simplicity, readability, and modularity.

To see this, take a look at a Python implementation of the hello world program, which prints the words `Hello World!`:

```
Print("Hello World!")
```

To do the same thing in Java, another popular programming language, we need something a bit more verbose:

```
System.out.println("Hello World!");
```

While this may not seem like a huge difference, extra research and consultation of documentation can add up, adding time to the data wrangling process.

Python also has built-in **data structures** that are relatively flexible in the way that they handle data.

 **Data structures** are abstractions that help organize the data in a program for easy manipulation. We will explore the various data structures in Python and R in `Chapter 2`, *Introduction to Programming in Python*.

This contributes to Python's relative ease of use, particularly when working with data on a low level.

Finally, because of Python's modularity and popularity within the scientific community, there are a number of **packages** built around Python that can be quite useful to us in data wrangling.

 **Packages/modules/libraries** are extensions of a language, or prewritten code in that language--typically built by individual users and the open source community--that add on functionality that is not built into the language. They can be **imported** in a program to include new tools. We will be leveraging packages throughout the book, both in R and Python, to extract, read, clean, shape, and store data.

# R

**R** is both a programming language and an environment built specifically for statistical computing. This definition has been taken from the R website, `r-project.org/about.html`:

> *The term 'environment' is intended to characterize [R] as a fully planned and coherent system, rather than an incremental accretion of very specific and inflexible tools, as is frequently the case with other data analysis software.*

In other words, one of the major differences between R and Python is that some of the most common functionalities for working with data--data handling and storage, visualization, statistical computation, and so on--come built in. A good example of this is **linear modeling,** a basic statistical method for modelling numerical data.

In R, linear modeling is a built-in functionality that is made very intuitive and straightforward, as we will see in `Chapter 5`, *Manipulating Text Data - An Introduction to Regular Expressions*. There are a number of ways to do linear modeling in Python, but they all require using external libraries and often doing extra work to get the data in the right format.

R also has a built-in data structure called a dataframe that can make manipulation of tabular data more intuitive.

The big takeaway here is that there are benefits and trade-offs to both languages. In general, being able to use the right tool for the job can save an immense amount of time spent on data wrangling. It is therefore quite useful as a data programmer to have a good working knowledge of each language and know when to use one or the other.

# Summary

This chapter has provided an overall context for the purpose, subject matter, and programming languages in this book. In summary, data wrangling is important because data in its original raw format is rarely prepared for its end use to begin with. Data wrangling involves getting and reading data, cleaning data, merging and shaping data, and storing data. In this book, data wrangling will be conducted using the R and Python programming languages.

In the next chapter, I will dive into Python, with an introduction to Python programming. I will introduce basic principals of programming and features of the Python language that will be used throughout the rest of the book. If you are already familiar with Python, you may want to skip ahead or skim through the following chapter.

In Chapter 3, *Reading, Exploring, and Modifying Data - Part I*, and Chapter 4, *Reading, Exploring, and Modifying Data - Part II*, I will take a generalized programming approach to data wrangling. Chapter 3, *Reading, Exploring, and Modifying Data - Part I*, and Chapter 4, *Reading, Exploring, and Modifying Data - Part II*, will discuss how to use Python programming to read, write, and manipulate data using Python.

# 2

# Introduction to Programming in Python

Programming is a powerful tool for manipulating data because it gives you the ability to build your own custom tools for tackling non standard problems. Much of the content in this book will make use of the Python programming language, so in this chapter, I will give a brief introduction to programming in python. The chapter will include the following topics:

- External resources
- Logistical overview
- Running programs in Python
- Data types, variables, and the Python shell
- Compound statements
- Making comments within programs
- A programmer's resources

If you are familiar with Python and general programming principals, you can comfortably skip ahead or skim through this chapter.

## External resources

Not everything can fit in to this book and some material is subject to change. I've made a number of resources available on the internet including the following:

- Installation instructions and guidelines
- Datasets for the exercises in the chapters

- Code from the exercises in the chapters
- Links to documentation, further reading, and other useful resources

All external resources are available in a shared Google Drive folder at `https://goo.gl/8S58ra`.

# Logistical overview

Each of the chapters will begin with a logistical overview, detailing the projects involved in the chapter, installation requirements, the file system setup for the projects and other useful details. These initial *Logistical Overview* sections will help you to get set up to follow along with the chapter.

In this chapter, I will walk through the creation of one Python program called `hello_world.py`. I will walk through the steps of creating the python program at the beginning of the chapter.

I will also introduce an interface for executing python commands directly called the terminal. Using the terminal, I will demonstrate several elementary programming concepts.

The finished product for the python program, as well as a program containing all of the terminal commands is available in the code folder of the external resources at `https://goo.gl/8S58ra`.

# Installation requirements

For this chapter, you will need the following:

- **Atom**, an open source text editor created by GitHub
- The latest version of **Python 3**

Links to installation instructions, and specific guidelines are made available in the *Installation* document in the external resources. Visit `https://goo.gl/8S58ra` and navigate to the *Installation* document. Within the installation document, the Atom and Python 3 installation links are under the *Chapter 3* header.

# Using other learning resources

In the *Links and Further Reading* document in the external resources, I've included links to some additional resources to learn Python. Some are a bit more interactive or more comprehensive then what I've provided here. There are plenty of great tutorials out there for Python, so if you do choose to go elsewhere for the basics, there are a couple of things to keep in mind:

- The code in this book is written Python 3 and not Python 2. Python 2 and Python 3 aren't that different, but if you learn Python 2 first, be prepared for some minor differences.
- The content of this book will require you to run Python on your local machine, so be sure to familiarize yourself with how to write and run code locally.
  Many online tutorials will have an interactive environment for you to work with in your browser; however, these tutorials will not cover the process of writing and running code in your own computer.

# Python 2 versus Python 3

At the time of writing this, Python 2 and Python 3 are both actively used; Python 2 is still taught in many tutorials, and a large number of forum discussions and blog posts on Python refer to Python 2. All this can make it confusing for beginners to decide which version to learn first. The reason for the confusion is that the adoption rate of Python 3 was relatively slow so Python 2 has been maintained longer than planned. However, Python 2 is set to be discontinued in 2020, which means that the core team that develops Python will no longer make updates to Python 2.

As Python 2 is on its way out, I will use Python 3 for this book. Despite a small number of strong opinions either way, Python 3 really isn't all that different. There are some minor syntactical and functional differences, but it's easy to learn them if you find yourself needing to use Python 2. (I've included some links in the reference material about these differences.)

# Running programs in python

A **programming language** is a set of syntactical rules to express instructions to the computer. These instructions are written in a **computer program**, a set of code that is stored in a static file in the file system of a computer.

In this section, you will make a simple program that prints the words `Hello World!` to the output. Completing this exercise will give you an introduction to the process of creating and running programs in Python.

# Using text editors to write and manage programs

Like any other practice, programming requires a certain set of tools.

The first of these is the **text editor**. Text editors for programming are not like ordinary word processors, which will often apply formatting to text and sometimes force users to save with certain file extensions. Programs need to be saved in a raw format in order to run properly. This can be done with plain text editors such as Notepad in Windows and gedit in Linux; however, there are a few reasons to use a specialized text editor to program:

- Code and data tend to be spread across multiple directories, so keeping things organized is an important part of programming. Specialized text editors will often include an interface to open, close, move around, and rename files in a particular directory.
- Programs have rigid syntax, so it can be hard to navigate, read, and write programs, and easy to make mistakes if there is nothing to reinforce that syntax. Specialized text editors will highlight the syntax of the programming language. They will also often include shortcuts to fill in common words and syntactical elements.

# Writing the hello world program

In the following steps, you will build your first python program:

1. Create an empty folder somewhere in your file system called `chapter2`. Once you have created the `chapter2` folder, open up Atom and add the folder to the file tree by selecting **File** | **Add Project Folder** as follows:

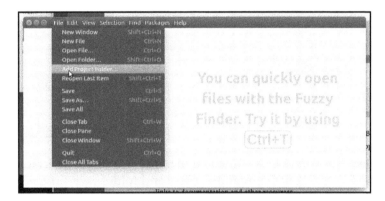

2. Navigate to the `chapter2` folder that you just created and click **OK**.
3. You should see the `chapter2` folder in the file tree, which is usually on the left panel. If the tree is not there, you may need to show it by selecting View | Toggle Tree View:

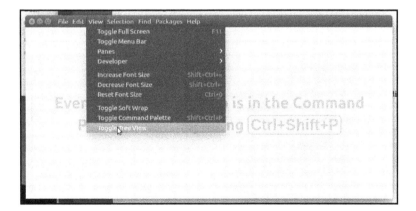

4. Within the `chapter2` folder, create a new file called `hello_world.py` by right-clicking on the `chapter2` folder from the file tree and selecting **New File**:

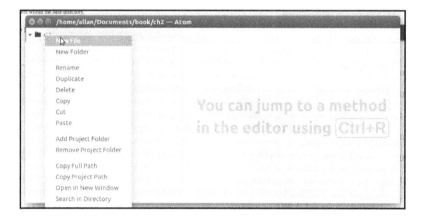

In general, you can use the file tree panel as a direct interface to create, delete, open, move and manage files and folders within the base directory.

5. Open `hello_world.py` by clicking on the file in the file tree. A blank text editing tab should open up for the file. Type the following text:

```
print("Hello World!")
```

6. Finally, save the file by selecting **File | Save**:

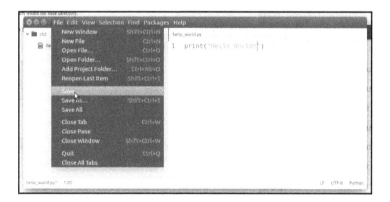

That's it! You've created your first program in Python! The next step is to execute the program.

# Using the terminal to run programs

The Terminal is an interface that allows the user to write instructions directly to the OS. You can use the Terminal to run the Python program that you just created. When running programs in the Terminal, the Terminal will display status and debugging messages produced by the program, which can be very useful.

Each operating system has its own version of the Terminal. To get started, open up the Terminal program for your operating system. In most distributions of Linux it is called **Terminal**, in Windows it is called Command Prompt, and in macOS it is called **shell**. Many of the commands also differ between operating systems; however, the commands that we will use in this book will be mostly the same irrespective of operating system. You should see a prompt in the upper left-hand corner that looks something like this:

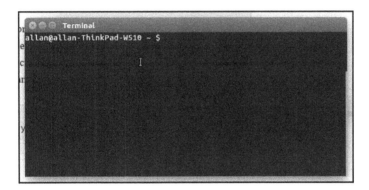

The first thing that you need to do to run your program is to navigate in the Terminal to the directory containing your program. Terminal commands take place within a specific folder in the computer's filesystem. Windows, Mac, and Linux all use the cd command, which stands for **change directory** and can be used to change the working directory. To change to the directory containing your hello_world.py file, you can use the following command:

```
$ cd <relative/path/to/directory>
```

A couple of things to note here:

When you see angle brackets in a Terminal command or a line of code, this often indicates a placeholder for something that is specific to your system or configuration. In the place of `<relative/path/to/directory>`, you will need to type the relative path to the folder containing your program (the `hello_world.py` file that you just created).

The `$` symbol indicates that the command should be entered into the Terminal and should not be copied with the rest of the command. Not all Terminal programs use a dollar symbol to indicate a prompt, so don't worry if yours doesn't look exactly like this.

The relative path to the directory refers to the exact sequence of folders leading from the current directory to the destination directory. The current directory is often listed at the beginning of each prompt. I the current directory is not listed at the beginning of the prompt, you can find it by using the `pwd` command in Linux and Mac.

The following command is used in Linux and Mac in order to show the current working directory:

```
$ pwd
```

The following is the command used in Windows to show the current working directory:

```
$ cd
```

In the relative path, each subsequent folder is separated by a forward slash (/) in Linux and Mac, and a backward slash (\) in Windows. The following is what it looks like on my computer to find the current directory, change to my `chapter2` folder, and then verify that I am in the correct location:

```
          Terminal
allan@allan-ThinkPad-W510 ~ $ pwd
/home/allan
allan@allan-ThinkPad-W510 ~ $ cd Documents/book/ch2/
allan@allan-ThinkPad-W510 ~/Documents/book/ch2 $ pwd
/home/allan/Documents/book/ch2
allan@allan-ThinkPad-W510 ~/Documents/book/ch2 $
```

If it is easier, you can also do this incrementally by changing folders one directory at a time. If you accidentally move to the wrong directory, you can use `..` to move up one directory in the filesystem:

```
$ cd ..
```

This command will change the working directory to the parent folder of the previous working directory. Another useful command for navigating files is the `ls` command in Mac and Linux, and the `dir` command in Windows. This command will list all of the files and folders in the current directory.

In Mac and Linux, the following command is used to list the contents of the current directory:

```
$ ls
```

In Windows the following command is used to list the contents of the current directory:

```
$ dir
```

# Running the Hello World program

In the following steps, I will walk through how to run a program using the terminal.

1. In your Terminal program, go ahead and change the working directory to the directory containing your `hello_world.py` program:

```
$ cd <relative/path/to/directory>
```

2. Verify that you are in the correct directory by using the appropriate command for your operating system. Once you have verified that you are in the correct directory, run the program by entering either of the following, depending on your setup:

```
$ python hello_world.py
$ python3 hello_world.py
```

Some operating systems will include a Python2 installation as `Python` and a Python3 installation as `python3`. There may be additional variations of the python command that are used by default. See the installation instructions in the external resources for more details.

3. Once you run the program, you should see printed out in your Terminal the words `Hello World!`. If you did, congratulations! You successfully ran your first program in Python:

```
Terminal
allan@allan-ThinkPad-W510 ~/Documents/book/ch2 $ python hello_world.py
Hello World!
allan@allan-ThinkPad-W510 ~/Documents/book/ch2 $
```

 This is what running the Hello World program looks like on my machine. Yours might be slightly different, so use the previous instructions, and not this, as a reference to run your program.

# What if it didn't work?

What if this didn't work? The first thing that you can do is to check over your syntax and see if you got something wrong. Step backward through your process to see where you might have made a mistake. You can look over the code that I have provided, both in the book and the external resources, but you shouldn't limit yourself to that. As a programmer, the internet is your best friend. If there is an error message, you can search for the error message and see if any forum threads come up. Chances are that somebody had the same problem you did. You can also see the notes at the end of this chapter about using documentation and online forums.

Debugging programs gets easier as you become more experienced, but making mistakes (and consequently receiving errors) is always a big part of programming no matter how experienced. It is very important to be comfortable investigating problems that come up, especially while starting out.

# Data types, variables, and the Python shell

In the next few sections, I will use a tool called the Python shell, which will help you get more comfortable using Python. The Python shell is a tool that allows the user to enter in Python commands, which get run instantaneously. This makes the Python shell a great place to quickly and easily experiment with small bits of code or new functionality in Python.

 There is no easy way of saving the code that is entered in the Python shell, so it is best to use it only for experimentation.

You can run the Python shell from a Terminal. To do this, open a Terminal and, from any directory, enter one of the following depending on your configuration:

```
$ Python
$ python3
```

You should see a new command prompt within the Terminal that looks something like this:

```
Terminal
allan@allan-ThinkPad-W510 ~/Documents/book/ch2 $ python3
Python 3.6.3 (default, Oct 28 2017, 06:26:02)
[GCC 5.4.0 20160609] on linux
Type "help", "copyright", "credits" or "license" for more information.
>>>
```

In Python, a single instruction is called a **simple statement**. For now, each individual line of code represents a simple statement. The Python shell will accept one line of code at a time. The following is an example of a simple statement that adds two numbers:

```
>> 1+1
```

Notice the **>>** at the beginning of our command. The **>>** symbol indicates that the line of code should be entered into the Python shell. The **>>** symbol should not be copied over with the rest of the code. You can run this statement by typing it into the shell and pressing *Enter*.

The Python shell will print out the result of every statement that you write. When you write the previous statement in your Python shell and press *Enter*, you should see the result of 2 printed just preceding it. The number 2 is an example of a value in Python. Values are like the nouns of programming languages. The + symbol is an example of an operator. Operators are like the verbs of programming languages, and they express what you would like to do with a value.

# Numbers - integers and floats

More specifically, the number 2 is an example of a value with an `int` data type or an integer value. An integer value can be any positive number, negative number, or zero without a trailing decimal point. A float value is any number with a trailing decimal point. To create a float value, you can simply write a decimal point after the number such as 1. or 1.5.

## Why integers?

It may seem peculiar at first to distinguish between `int` and `float` as fundamentally different data types. The first reason to make the distinction is that computers store these numbers differently and, for the sake of computer programming, there are a couple of scenarios in which it makes more sense for a programming language to use one or the other. For example, as we will see later in this chapter, using a `float` to index an array will cause an error and thus prevent the program from running.

 If you find yourself using Python 2, you may notice that the interpreter treats arithmetic differently for integers than it does for floats, rounding the results, which can lead to some unexpected errors.

You can add, divide, and multiply in a single statement, using the same rules you would expect in a scientific calculator. The order of operations is as follows:

1. Expressions inside parentheses.
2. Exponents.
3. Division.
4. Multiplication.
5. Addition and subtraction.

The following commands are some examples of arithmetic in Python:

```
>> 2 * 3
>> 4 + 5 / 6
>> (4 + 5) / 6
>> ( ( 1 * 2 ) / 3 / 4 ) + 5 - (6 / 5)
```

Exponents in Python are denoted using two consecutive multiplication ** symbols. Careful not to use the ^ symbol for exponentiation in Python. The following is an example of arithmetic in python:

```
>> 3 ** 2
```

 **Implicit conversion**: You might have noticed that all of the previous operations use integers, but sometimes yield floats as results. This is because the Python interpreter changes the data type of the values just before the operation so that you get a result that makes intuitive sense. This is called **implicit conversion** and it is one of the things that makes Python so easy to use and beginner friendly. However, implicit conversion doesn't always happen, so it is important to keep track of the data types that you are using throughout your program.

# Strings

A value with a string data type is simply a collection of characters. You've already seen a `string` data type in use from the hello world program that you created earlier, namely, `Hello World!`. String values are created in Python by writing the contents of a string inside quotation marks:

```
>> "your string here"
```

Two or more strings can be merged together or concatenated using the + operator:

```
>> "string 1 " + "string 2"
```

Python does not distinguish between single quotes and double quotes; however, the opening quotes must be the same as the closing quotes (`"This will not work'`).

I will cover string operations in detail in `Chapter 5`, *Manipulating Text Data - An Introduction to Regular Expressions*.

# Booleans

The Boolean data type has two, and only two, possible values, namely, `True` and `False`. In Python, you can produce a Boolean value by writing either `True` or `False`, starting with a capital T or F respectively:

```
>> True
>> False
```

Boolean values can be combined using bitwise operators:

- The `and` operator yields `True` if the value on the left and the value on the right are both `True`
- The `or` operator yields `True` if at least one of the items on the left or right is `True`

The following are some examples using bitwise operators:

```
>> True and True
>> True and False
>> True or False
>> False or False
```

Logical operators can be used to produce Boolean values from other data types by comparing values:

- The `==` operator yields `True` if the values on either side are equal
- The `>` operator yields `True` if value to the left is greater than the value to the right
- The `<` operator yields `True` if the value to the right is greater than the value to the left

The following are some examples using logical operators:

```
>> 1 == 2
>> 1 == 1
>> 1 < 2
>> 1 < 0
>> 1 > 2
>> 2 > 1
>> "abc" == "abc"
>> "abc" == "cba"
```

Boolean values are good to make decisions within computer programs. You will see this when I introduce **if statements** later in the chapter. They are also good to store simple yes/no data entries, such as whether a particular individual lives in New York or whether a transaction has been completed.

# The print function

I've been taking it for granted so far that the Python shell automatically prints the result of any statement that is entered. However, if you want to see the result of a particular operation inside a Python program, you will need to explicitly print it using the print() function. To use the print() function, you can type print() with the value that you would like to print inside parentheses.

Here are some examples using the print() function:

```
or example:>> print(0)
>> print(1+1)
>> print('abc')
>> print("abc" == "cba")
```

The syntax used with the print function may seem a bit strange right now, but it will become more clear when I introduce functions later in the chapter.

There are two areas that the print() function comes in handy. The first of these is to test and debug programs. In order to see whether your program is working properly, or why it is not working properly, it is helpful to look inside the program while it is running. You can do this by placing print() functions in the program where you want to investigate what is happening. To give a really basic example, if a program that outputs a number produces the wrong number, one approach is to print the number at various stages of the program to identify where things go wrong.

The second use of `print()` functions is to track the progress or status of a program. Processing large datasets can often take a really long time, so it can be helpful to have some sense of how far along the program is and how long it might take to finish. For example, when processing a large dataset row by row, it can be helpful to print out the fraction of rows that have been processed.

# Variables

In order to make effective programs, you will need to store values that you can access and modify across multiple lines of code. In Python, you can store a value using a variable. A variable is a sequence of characters that is made to represent some value in the program. To create a variable, you can use the assignment (=) operator. The assignment operator takes the value to the right and assigns it to the variable name on the left. The following statements will create a variable called `myVariable` and print it out:

```
>> myVariable = 1
>> print(myVariable)
```

It can be easy when starting out to confuse the assignment = operator with the logical equal "==" operator. Make a mental note that a single = is the assignment operator and a double '==' is the logical equal operator.

After a variable is created, using the name of a variable in a statement is the same as using the value that the variable contains. The following are some examples of statements that use variables:

```
>> myVariable = 4
>> print(myVariable+2)
>> myVariable = "abc"+"cba"
>> print(myVariable+"abc")
>> myVariable = True
>> print(myVariable and True)
```

**Dynamic typing**: In many languages, the value assigned to a variable needs to have a specific data type that is specified when the variable is created. However, this is not the case in Python. A value with any data type can be assigned to any variable. This is referred to as **dynamic typing**.

You can also change a variable relative to its own value. This is sometimes called **incrementing** (in the case of addition) or **decrementing** (in the case of subtraction):

```
>> myVariable = 0
>> myVariable = myVariable + 5
>> print(myVariable)
```

There is a shorthand for changing a variable based on its own value that can be used for addition, subtraction, multiplication and division. The following examples demonstrate how changing the value of a variable can be expressed more concisely. First, the following creates a variable and sets it to 0:

```
>> myVariable = 0.
```

# Adding to a variable

To increase the value of a variable, you can use the += symbol as follows:

```
>> myVariable += 5.
>> print(myVariable)
```

The value of myVariable is now 5.

# Subtracting from a variable

To subtract from a variable, you can use the -= symbol as follows:

```
>> myVariable -= 2.
>> print(myVariable)
```

The value of myVariable is now 3.

# Multiplication

To multiply a variable by a value, you can use the *= symbol as follows:

```
>> myVariable *= 6.
>> print(myVariable)
```

The value of myVariable is now 18.

# Division

To divide a variable by a value, you can use the /= symbol as follows:

```
>> myVariable /= 3.
>> print(myVariable)
```

The value of `myVariable` is now 6.

# Naming variables

Using the right name for a variable is important. There are some conventions and some syntactical rules to name variables properly. Variables have to be one word, they have to start with a letter or underscore, and all remaining characters must be a letter, a number, or an underscore. If these rules are not followed, the program will produce an error.

There are two best practices to take into account when choosing a variable name. First, the variable name should reflect its function in the program. This makes it easier to keep track of how the program functions. Second, if the variable name consists of several words, these should be separated using either camel case or snail case to make it easier to read.

In camel case, the first word starts with a lowercase letter, while all the following words start with an uppercase letter. In snail case, each word is lowercase and is separated by an underscore. It is best practice to use either one or the other for a given program and stick with it, though this can get tricky, especially if multiple people are working on the same project.

Variables are a key part of what makes programming an effective means of expression. Storing and labeling data can make it easier to reference and keep track of, but it also makes it possible to build more sophisticated operations. This will become clear when I introduce compound statements later in this chapter.

# Arrays (lists, if you ask Python)

An array is an ordered collection of values. Each item in an array is called an **element**. In Python, there can be an indefinite number of elements in an array. Python has a special name for its implementation of arrays, called a **list**. With regard to Python, I will use both words to refer to the same thing.

The following syntax can be used to create an array:

```
<arrayName>=[<element1>,<element2>,<element3>,...]
```

Inside square brackets, each element in the array is listed, separated by commas:

```
>> myArray = ["foo","bar","sup?","yo!"]
>> print(myArray)
```

The elements of an array can be accessed by their relative position, or index, in the array. To access an element of an array, you can use the following syntax:

```
>> <arrayName>[<index>]
```

For example:

```
>> print(myArray[0])
>> thirdElement = myArray[2]
>> print(thirdElement)
```

You may have noticed that the index of the third element of the array is 2, and not 3. This is because indexing starts with zero in Python and many other languages. This can be a bit confusing when starting out. When indexing arrays, be sure to access the nth element of an array using the number, n-1. Also notice that the index of the array has an integer data type. If you try to access an array with a float value, it will cause an error even if it represents an integer number (that is, 1.0).

You can also set the value of a particular element of an array by assigning a value to its index. The following line will set the first element of myArray to the string, I'm a new value:

```
>> myArray[0] = "I'm a new value"
>> print myArray[0]
```

You can only access or set a value of an array if the index belongs to the array. The following two lines will generate an error, because the array only has four elements, so its maximum index is three (for the fourth element):

```
>> myArray[6]
>> myArray[4]
```

Arrays are useful to represent grouped collections of data like a row in a spreadsheet. By keeping track of a set of data items in an ordered list, it is possible to easily store and retrieve items from a grouped collection of data.

# Dictionaries

A **dictionary**, like an array, is a collection of items; however, the items in a dictionary are referenced by strings called **keys**, rather than their order in a list. Another way to think of a dictionary is as a collection of key-value pairs, where the keys are used to retrieve the values.

To create a dictionary, use the following syntax where <key1>, <key2> are strings and value1, value2 are any values:

```
{<key1>:<value1>,<key2>:<value2>,<key3>:<value3>}
```

Notice that a dictionary has curly brackets whereas an array has square brackets.

The following line will create a dictionary called d with two key-value pairs:

```
>> d = {"some_number": 1, "sup?": "yo!"}
>> print(d)
```

You can access a specific value of a dictionary using the following syntax:

```
<dictionary name>[<key>]
```

For example:

```
>> print(d["sup?"])
>> print(d["some_number"])
```

You can also set the value of a key by assigning a value to that key, as the following demonstrates:

```
>> d["some_number"] = 5
>> print(d["some_number"])
```

If you assign a value to a key that does not yet exist in a particular dictionary, the key will be added to the dictionary:

```
>> d["new_key"] = "I'm a new value"
>> print(d["new_key"])
```

On an intuitive level, the big advantage of Python dictionaries comes from the ability to store and reference items by key. It is easier to remember a name than a number. If, for example, you are working with a spreadsheet that has 100 columns, it is much more convenient to retrieve an entry by its column header than its position.

# Compound statements

So far, each line of code that you have written gets executed exactly once and immediately after it is written. Compound statements are Python structures that allow you to control when and how certain pieces of code get executed. Compound statements significantly increase your expressiveness as a programmer. In other words, they allow you to do more with less code. Before introducing a few compound statements, it will be helpful to go over the syntactical structure.

# Compound statement syntax and indentation level

A compound statement consists of two parts. The first part, the **clause header**, is a line containing the type of statement and some other information specific to the statement. The clause header always starts with the type of clause and ends with a colon. The following is the syntax of a clause header:

```
<clause type> <clause body>:
```

(Note that this figure and the next two are just to demonstrate the syntactical structure and do not represent functional code).

The second part is called the **suite** in the documentation, but it is also called a **code block**, which is the term I will use in this book. The code block is a series of additional statements that are controlled by the compound statement. Each statement belonging to the code block should have four additional spaces before, as compared to the clause header. The additional four spaces are called a level of indentation:

```
<clause header>:
    <I'm a line of code in the code block...>
    <another line in the code block...>
    <yet another line of code, also in the code block...>
<I'm a line of code, but I'm not in the code block...>
```

Tabs versus spaces: Formally, a level of indentation refers to the exact number of tabs and spaces that come before a particular statement. The Python interpreter will recognize any number of tabs and/or spaces as an indentation level so long as all the statements in a code block share the same number and order of tabs and spaces. Of course, it is never a good idea to mix tabs and spaces as this can get confusing fast. However, some programmers do prefer to use tabs rather than spaces to indicate indentation level. In this book, I will strictly use four spaces for each indentation level as that is the default for the Atom text editor.

There can be additional compound statements within the code block of another compound statement, so there are usually multiple levels of indentation used in a Python program:

```
<Clause header>:
    <I'm a line of code in the code block...>
    <another line in the code block...>
    <yet another line of code, also in the code block...>
    <Clause Header #2>:
        <code block #2>
<I'm a line of code, but I'm not in the code block...>
```

In the previous example, `Clause header #2` and `code block #2` represent a compound statement that is placed within the first compound statement.

The Atom text editor, and many others like it, makes it quite easy to keep track of the indentation level when working with Python (`.py`) files. When the *Tab* key is pressed, the cursor will snap forward to a number of spaces that is a multiple of four. When the *Backspace* key is pressed, the cursor will go back four spaces. (Note that for this to work, the file has to be named with a `.py` extension.)

An easy way to experiment with this is by making a file called `tabs.py` in your `chapter2` folder and pressing *Tab*, spacebar, and *Backspace* multiple times. Note that the formatting will not work until the file is saved as a `.py` file. Here is an example of using tabs and spaces in a Python file:

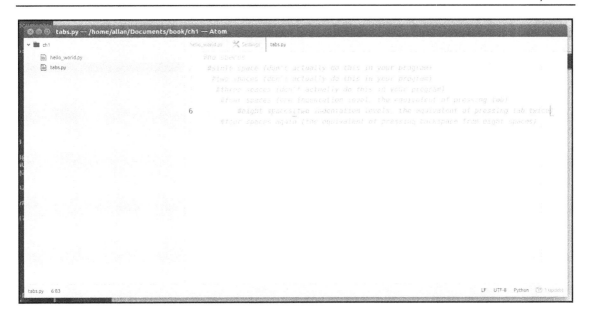

I will be using a text editor to write the remainder of the examples. If you are following along with the code, I recommend that you write the following examples in the text editor and run it from the terminal, as you did in the beginning of the chapter.

# For statements and iterables

A `for` statement is a compound statement that allows you to run a code block repeatedly a fixed number of times. For loops go hand in hand with Python structures called **iterables**. An iterable contains or references a sequence of items in a fixed order. Both arrays and strings are examples of iterables in Python.

The clause header of a for statement contains a variable name and an iterable, and follows the following syntax:

```
for <variable name> in <iterable>:
    <code block>
```

Each time the code block of a for statement is run, Python will create the variable named in the clause header and assign to it the value of the next item in the iterable. The for statement ends when there are no more items left in the iterable. In this way, it is possible to perform the same operation *for* each item in an iterable.

To give a concrete example, the following program will create an array called `colors` and print out each color in the array one by one:

```
colors = ['red','orange','blue']
for color in colors:
    print(color)
```

This is the equivalent of writing the following:

```
colors = ['red','orange','blue']
color = colors[0]
print color
color = colors[1]
print color
color = colors[2]
```

It is easy to see why this is useful. If you need to perform an operation on each element of an array that has 1,000 entries, a `for` loop can save you at least 2,000 lines of code. Repetitive code takes more time to write, but it also makes your program harder to read, harder to update, and more prone to error.

Most of the tasks that clean and modify data involve performing some kind operation on each of the entries in a dataset. Making effective use of for statements is therefore a key part of data wrangling.

# If statements

An `if` statement is a compound statement that allows you to run a block of code conditionally. This means that if a certain condition is met, the code will run; otherwise, it will not. If statements have the following syntax:

```
if <booleanValue>:
    <code block>
```

The Boolean value in the clause header is the condition of the if statement. If the Boolean value is `True`, then the code block is run. If the Boolean value is `False`, then the code block is not run. In the following example, the program will print "Nice Weather!" if the value of the `isSunny` variable is `True`:

```
isSunny = True
if isSunny:
    print("Nice Weather!")
```

In the next example, the value of isSunny is changed to False, so nothing will happen:

```
isSunny = False
if isSunny:
>      print("Nice Weather!")
```

# Else and elif clauses

The combination of a single clause header and a code block is called a **clause**. Some compound statements, including the if statement, are able to have multiple clauses.

The elif clause (short for else if) follows directly after the initial if clause. If the condition of the if clause is not met, the elif clause will check to see whether a second condition is met, and conditionally run another block of code. The following program uses an elif clause to check whether it is cloudy when it is not sunny:

```
isSunny = False
isCloudy = True
if isSunny:
    print('Nice Weather!')
elif isCloudy:
    print('Might Rain Soon!')
```

An if statement must start with an if clause, but there can be an indefinite number of elif clauses chained one after the other. If the condition of the if clause is met, the first block of code will run. If the condition of the next elif clause is met, the second code block will run. If the condition of the next elif clause is met, the second code block will run, and so on.

The following example demonstrates how this is composed syntactically:

```
if <first condition>:
    <first code block>
elif <second condition>:
    <second code block>
elif <third condition>:
    <third code block>
. . . .
```

An `else` clause can be written at the end of an if statement. If none of the conditions for any of the previous clauses are met, the code block of the else clause will run. The following program will print out `Not much going on with the weather right now`, because the conditions for all of the previous clauses in the if statement are false:

```
isSunny=False
isCloudy=False
isRaining=False
if isSunny:
    print("Nice Weather!")
elif isCloudy:
    print("Might rain soon!")
elif isRaining:
    print("I should bring my umbrella!")
else:
    print("Not much going on with the weather right now...")
```

 Try experimenting with different combinations of true and false for the Boolean variables that are created at the beginning of the previous program.

# Functions

A function is a labeled block of code that can be used at any point throughout the program. A function in Python follows the following syntax:

```
def <nameOfFunction>(<parameters>):
    <code block>
```

Notice the parentheses following the name of the function. Inside the parentheses, it is possible to specify certain variables called **parameters** or **arguments**. I will get back to this shortly, but for now, you can ignore the `<parameters>` bit as it is optional. The following program creates a simple function that will print the words `Nice Weather!` to the Terminal:

```
def reactToTheWeather():
    print("Nice Weather!")
```

If you run the previous example, you will notice that nothing in particular happens. This is because the code block of a function is only executed if and when you tell the program to do so. When the code block of a function is used by the program, it is called executing or calling the function. To call a function, simply write the name of the function, followed by an open and closed parentheses. In the following example, I've modified the `nice_weather` program to call the `reactToTheWeather` function three times:

```
def reactToTheWeather():
    print("Nice Weather!")

reactToTheWeather()
reactToTheWeather()
reactToTheWeather()
```

After running the previous program, you should now see the words `Nice Weather!` printed to the Terminal three times:

It is possible, and often quite useful, to write compound statements within other compound statements. In the following example, I have placed an if statement inside the `reactToTheWeather` function:

```
def reactToTheWeather():
    isSunny = True
    if isSunny:
        print("Nice Weather!")

reactToTheWeather()
```

## Passing arguments to a function

If you look at the previous example, you might notice that the if statement inside the function doesn't really do much. According to the function, the value of the `isSunny` variable is always `True`. Ideally, the `reactToTheWeather` function should be able to change its behavior based on some outside information, specifically whether or not it is sunny.

When calling a function, it is possible to pass in values called arguments or parameters from outside the function. The names of the arguments that should be made available to the function are written using the following syntax:

```
def <function name>(<argument1>,<argument2>,<argument3>):
    <code block>

<function name>(<value1>,<value2>,<value3>)
```

When the function is called, the values for each of the arguments are written inside the parentheses, separated by commas. The arguments are then made available to the code block of a function as variables with the names specified in the clause header.

The following is an example to demonstrate how this works in practice. In the following example, the `reactToTheWeather` function is changed to accept one argument called `isSunny`. When the `reactToTheWeather` function is called, the value for the `isSunny` argument is passed in. When the code block runs, the `isSunny` variable takes on the value that was passed in when the function was called:

```
def reactToTheWeather(isSunny):
    if isSunny:
        print("Nice Weather!")
    else:
        print("No sun today!")
```

```
reactToTheWeather(True)
reactToTheWeather(False)
```

# Returning values from a function

In addition to passing in information when a function is executed, it is also possible to retain information afterward using the **return statement**. A return statement is simply the word, **return**, followed by the value to be returned, and is written at the end of the code block:

```
def myFunction():
    <some code>
    return <return value>
```

The return value is captured outside of the function by assigning the function call to a variable. In the following example, I've modified the code slightly to print the reaction to the weather outside of the function:

```
def reactToTheWeather(isSunny):
    if isSunny:
        return "Nice Weather!"
    else:
        return "No sun today!"

reaction1 = reactToTheWeather(True)
print(reaction1)
reaction2 = reactToTheWeather(True)
print(reaction1)
```

# Making annotations within programs

A **comment** or **annotation** is a piece of text inside a program that has no effect on the program. Comments are used to make notes about the code itself for those reading it. A comment is made simply by writing some text after the # character:

```
# I'm a comment, I have no impact on the function of the program
# but provide useful information about the code.
# This code prints the words 'Hello World!' to the output...
print('Hello World!')
```

Annotations are useful for two reasons. First, annotations can help others understand what your code does and how it functions. However, even if you don't need to collaborate or share your work, annotations are very helpful in helping you mentally organize your own work. This is especially useful if you end up needing to reuse a piece of code weeks or months after writing it.

# A programmer's resources

The art of programming is the art of constantly learning. Every new framework, paradigm, and programming challenge can present a need to learn something new. While there's no one formula for how to keep up to date with trends and tackle new problems, two resources in particular will be instrumental to being an effective programmer.

## Documentation

Whenever starting out with a new language or package, the first thing to look for is the documentation. Good documentation usually contains information on how to get started, examples and use cases, and most importantly, references that will tell you how to use the *language/package/tool*. You can often find the documentation you are looking for by searching *<name of language or package> documentation*. Documentation is often the first line of defense in learning how to do what you want with a certain programming tool. The documentation for Python, for example, can be found at `https://docs.Python.org`.

## Online forums and mailing lists

Programmers can be quite generous in offering help and support to others starting out; however, be sure to be polite and respectful. When debugging an error, trying to figure out how to go about doing something: or trying to understand how a particular feature works, **online forums** can be quite helpful.

A good example of an online forum is Stack Overflow, where users can post questions to a large community of developers of varying levels of experience. In addition, the developers of a given package will often have a mailing list where they will offer help to users trying to use the package. This is a good place to go if, for example, it is unclear from the documentation how to do exactly what you want.

A general rule of thumb when looking for help from others is that if you are being inefficient with other people's time, you probably aren't using your own time that well either. Before seeking help, it's good practice to do what you can to try to understand and solve the problem on your own. Make sure you look through your code thoroughly to see if you can identify an error; if it's not too hard, consult the documentation to look for your solution and search for previous posts that may answer your question. When looking for help, be as specific as possible about the problem you are trying to solve or the question that you have, and follow the guidelines of whatever forum or mailing list you are using (they are probably similar to what I've mentioned earlier).

# Summary

In this chapter, we went through the basics of Python programming, but we've also started to cover conceptually some of the fundamentals to create, store, and work with data. If you've made it this far, give yourself a pat on the back. You've successfully created your first program and learned the syntax of the Python programming language.

In the next chapter, you will take some of these principals to the next level to continue your data wrangling journey. I will talk first about modules, which allow you to add previously written code with additional functionality to our program. You will use modules to read from and write to different files, or conduct file I/O. I will cover the usage of *for statements* to iterate through the entries of a dataset, and basic methods to analyze and modify the data. Finally, I will cover functions that allow us to create blocks of code that we can run several times.

# 3
# Reading, Exploring, and Modifying Data - Part I

Even if you are new to programming, opening, modifying and saving files within programs should be a relatively familiar process. You have likely opened and edited a document with a word processor or entered data into an Excel spread sheet.

Like a computer program, a dataset can be represented using a text file with a specific syntactical structure. The text in a data file specifies both the information contained in the data and the structure in which that information is placed. In a sense, writing a program to process data files is a similar to the process of editing a document or a spreadsheet. First, the content of a file is opened, observed, and modified, and then the result is saved.

 Another general strategy to store and retrieve digital data is to use a database. Databases are organized collections of data that allow for efficient storage, retrieval, and modification. I will revisit databases in `Chapter 9`, *Working with Large Datasets*.

The major difference between processing a data file in Python and editing a spreadsheet in Excel is that programming tools give you much more fine tuned control over the way in which the information is processed. In this way, programming gives you the flexibility to build custom tools for specific tasks as you need them.

Approaches to programming range from **highly specific** to **highly expressive**. In the context of data wrangling, this means that data processing tasks that are relatively unusual or complicated may require a more customized set of programming instructions (*highly specific*). Here are just a few examples of tasks that may require a more *specific* approach:

- Processing significantly large amounts of data
- Processing data in a hierarchical format

- Processing obscure data formats
- Restructuring data or converting between formats
- Extracting information from a body of text or data without well defined structure

By contrast, data processing tasks that are relatively routine or simple may be best be approached with an existing set of programming tools that can express a sequence of actions more concisely (*highly expressive*). Here are some examples of tasks that may benefit from a more *expressive* approach:

- Filtering out **data entries** based on the values that they contain.
- Selecting and extracting certain **variables**
- Aggregating the values of particular **variables**
- Creating new **variables** based off of existing ones

 A **data entry** is an individual observation in a dataset, also called a record, document or row. A **variable**, also called an attribute or column refers to a data variable in the dataset.

Because data challenges come in all shapes and sizes, it helps to have to have a sense for both ends of the spectrum so that you can choose the best tool for the job. I will start in this chapter with a rather low level (*specific*) overview of the steps involved in processing a data file programmatically. This chapter will include the following sections:

- External resources
- Logistical overview
- Introducing a basic data wrangling work flow
- Introducing the JSON file format
- Opening and closing a file in Python using file I/O
- Reading the contents of a file

# External resources

Not everything can fit in to this book and some material is subject to change. I've made a number of resources available on the internet including the following:

- Installation instructions and guidelines
- Datasets for the exercises in the chapters
- Code from the exercises in the chapters

- Links to documentation, further reading, and other useful resources

All external resources are available in a shared google drive folder at `https://goo.gl/ 8S58ra`.

# Logistical overview

In this chapter, I will do a demonstration of a single program called `process_data.py`. The `process_data.py` program will read a JSON file containing the data for this chapter, extract some of the variables from the data and output a new dataset to an output JSON file.

At the end of the chapter, I will demonstrate an alternative version of `process_data.py` called `process_data2.py` that allows for external specification of the input and output filenames.

The finished product for all of the code is available in the code folder of the external resources. All external resources are available at the following link: `https://goo.gl/ 8S58ra`.

# Installation requirements

For this chapter, you will need the following:

- **Atom**, an open source text editor created by GitHub
- The latest version of **Python 3**

Links and guidelines for all of the installation requirements are made available in the *Installation* a part of the reference material. Visit `https://goo.gl/8S58ra` and find the Atom and Python 3 headlines for installation links and instructions.

# Data

In this chapter, I will be using a dataset from Seeclickfix, a platform to report non-emergency issues to local governments. The dataset contains a series of data entries that represent issue reports that were made using the Seeclickfix platform. The dataset for this chapter is available for download from the *data* folder of the external resources.

# File system setup

To follow along with the demonstrations in this chapter, you should create a project folder to contain the Python scripts called `ch3`. The `ch3` folder should contain the code for this chapter, along with a folder to contain the data, called `data`. The `data` folder should contain the `scf_data.json` file used in this chapter. The following outlines the directory structure used:

```
ch3
--> process_data.py
--> process_data2.py
--> data/
----> scf_data.json
```

# Introducing a basic data wrangling work flow

This chapter is about understanding the components of a program that processes data. As mentioned in the introduction, the approach taken here will be to process data on a basic level. A particular emphasis is placed on opening, reading and writing data in this chapter. Later chapters will focus more on exploration and modification of data.

The following is a basic work flow for data wrangling that applies to processing data files. Data wrangling is not necessarily a linear process, but these steps will help to give a frame of reference for the range of tools and approaches that will be demonstrated in this chapter and throughout the rest of the book.

1. Open the file containing the input data from within the program:
   - In order for a program to gain access to the data in a particular file, the program first needs to interact with the computer's file system to open the file. This is referred to as file I/O and Python has built-in support to make this process relatively simple.

2. Read the data into the program:
   - Once the file is open, the next step is to read the raw text in the data file into the program's memory and convert the data to a programmatic data structure. Steps 1 and 2 are often combined though it is helpful to think of them separately regardless.

3. Explore the contents of the file:
   - It is usually necessary to do some exploration of the data in order to know what needs to be cleaned, extracted, or changed and how to do this. This is also sometimes called **auditing** the data.

4. Modify the contents of the file:
   - The data should be cleaned, processed, and/or shaped so that the output is ready for its end use.

5. Output the modified data to a new file:
   - The processed data should output to a new file to store for further analysis or data wrangling.

# Introducing the JSON file format

If you have worked with an Excel spreadsheet, you are already familiar with one type of data file. A spreadsheet is an example of data with a **tabular** format. In a tabular dataset, the entries are arranged as a series of rows and columns, where each column represents a data variable and each row represents a data entry. In Chapter 4, *Reading, Exploring, and Modifying Data - Part II*, you will work with **CSV** files, a form of tabular data.

The dataset for this chapter uses the **JSON** file format. JSON is an example of a **hierarchical** data format. Hierarchical data is more free-form than tabular data, though usually a JSON dataset will contain a series of data entries with a fixed structure.

JSON has two structures that have the same form as the Python dictionary and the Python array. The first of these structures is a collection of key value pairs, while the other is a collection of ordered values. Each of the values can be either an individual data element or an additional nested structure. This allows for an indefinitely nested set of structures and data elements. The following is a section of the JSON dataset used with this chapter:

```
},
"updated_at": "2017-08-2(
"closed_at": null,
"shortened_url": null,
"flag_url": "https://seed
"url": "https://seeclick
"reopened_at": null,
"lng": -74.0420227050781,
"html_url": "https://seed
"id": 3662906,
"address": "467 Manila A
"description": "This one
"summary": "Streets: Pot
"acknowledged_at": null,
"rating": 1,
"media": {
    "image_square_100x100
    "representative image
    "image_full": "https
    "video_url": null
},
```

You can see from the screenshot that JSON is not only structurally similar to python but also syntactically quite similar. Because the structure of JSON corresponds to Python dictionaries and lists, it is simple and intuitive to represent a JSON file in Python. In the remainder of the chapter, I will walk through some basic steps for opening, reading and processing JSON data in python.

# Opening and closing a file in Python using file I/O

In order to gain access to a file, a computer program needs to interact with the operating system; the process is called **file I/O**. File I/O is the way in which a programming language is able to open, read from, write to, and close files. (The I/O here stands for input/output, because the program takes input from certain files and writes output to other files.)

While it is not always necessary to explicitly open a file, it is important to conceptually separate the process of opening a file from the process of reading the contents of a file. This is because it is often necessary to read the contents of a file incrementally or specify particular parameters when the file is opened.

In the following subsection, I will show to use python to open a file.

# The open function and file objects

To open a file, you can use Python's built-in `open()` function:

```
file = open("<relative/path/to/file>", "<permission>")
```

The variable named `file` in the previous example is what the documentation calls a `file` object. A `file` object doesn't actually contain the contents of the file, rather it is used to access the file's location in memory and give the program permission to operate on the file. The `file` object is generally used as a parameter to other functions that read the data.

The first parameter of the `open()` function is a string containing the relative path from the directory in which the program is run to the file containing your data.

The second parameter is the permission, which is a string designating the level of permission that is granted to the program for working with a file. I will use two permissions in this book for file I/O:

- The read permission, designated by the `r` character, allows the program to read, but not to modify the contents of the file
- The write permission, designated by the `w` character, allows the program to write to the file and automatically erases the contents of any file that already exists with the specified file path

There's a good reason not to use the `'w'` permission unless you really intend to write to a particular file. Typically, in file browsers, there are precautions to make sure you do not lose data accidentally. If you are about to delete a file, a dialogue might come up to confirm, or the file might be moved temporarily to a trash bin folder before being permanently deleted.

When opening a file with the `'w'` permission, Python will mercilessly overwrite any file that already exists with the file path specified. As such, it is always a good idea to double-check that you are opening your data to read with the `'r'` position and back up your input and output data.

# File structure - best practices to store your data

The file structure for this chapter was outlined in the logistics section, but I will go over it again here in order to make a few points. It is convenient to keep all of your data and code in the same folder so that you can easily keep track of where everything is for a particular project. I like to go a step further and put all of the data in another folder within the project folder. The following is the directory structure I will be using in this chapter:

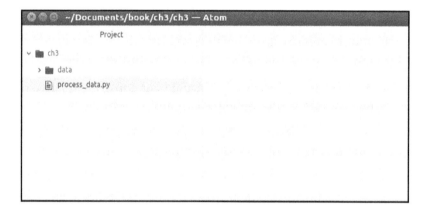

There is a practical reason for the separate data folder beyond mental organization. In Atom and many other text editors, accidentally opening a data file that is too large can crash the text editor. Keeping the data files in an entirely separate directory helps you avoid accidentally clicking on and opening a data file instead of a code file.

The exact directory structure that you choose for a given project should vary depending on the specifics of the project. For example, I will sometimes subdivide my data folder when working with multiple different data sources. I also sometimes include an additional directory for my code when I use several code files in the same project.

You may also hear of something called version control (that is, Git). Version control is a method to keep track of changes to a code base. I won't be using version control in this book, but if you do find yourself needing to use version control for a data wrangling project, note that it is important not to include large data files in the tracking. Keeping all of the data files in a separate location makes.

# Opening a file

In this subsection, you will perform the following:

1. Create and organize a project folder for data wrangling.
2. Place your data in the project folder.
3. Write a program to open and close a data file.

In later sections, you will build on this program to read and process the data. The following steps will guide you through the process of setting up your file system and opening the data file.

1. Open Atom. If you have another text editor that you prefer, you may use that one. Create a project folder called ch3 and add the project folder to the file tree. Inside the ch3 folder, create a file called process_data.py. Additionally, inside the ch3 folder, add an additional folder called data:

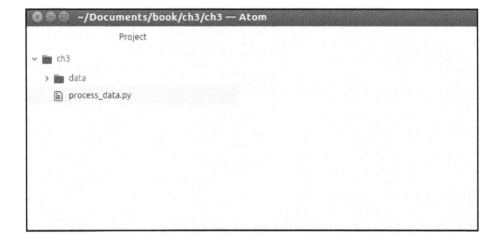

2.  If you haven't already, download the `scf_data.json` file from the *data* folder of the reference material and place the data in your `data` folder:

3. In your `process_data.py` file, use the `open()` function to open `scf_data.JSON` with read (`'r'`) permission:

```
inFile = open("data/scf_data.json",'r')
```

Note that if you are using Windows, there is an important difference to keep in mind when writing relative path strings in Python. Windows uses the backslash \ character to separate folder names in a file path, while macOS and Linux use the forward slash / character. However, a backslash character in Python is used for another purpose, so in Windows you will need to write two backslashes \\ in order to separate folders. The following is the Windows version:

```
inFile = open("data\\scf_data.json",'r')
```

I will be using the macOS/Linux version to create file paths in future programs, so be sure to change this if you are using Windows.

4. It is good practice to explicitly close the file when you are done using it. You can do this using the `file` object's `close()` function:

```
inFile = open("data/scf_data.json",'r')
inFile.close()
```

5. Next, I'm going to jump ahead a bit, just to prove that the previous example does something useful. In the following continuation of `process_data.py`, you will use the `read()` function of the `file` object to read and print the raw contents of the data file:

```
inFile = open("data/scf_data.json",'r')
print(inFile.read())
inFile.close()
```

6. Go ahead and run the previous file. You should see the raw data from the file printed to the output:

# Reading the contents of a file

A data file, like Python code, is simply a collection of text that follows a set of syntactical rules. In order for a Python program to make use of the data in the data file, it has to be converted to a data structure that can be processed programmatically.

**Reading** a file typically refers to the process a program uses to collect raw data, while converting data from a raw text format to a data structure is called **parsing** the data. The term *reading a file* can also refer to both collecting and parsing data. Usually, there are tools that take care of reading and parsing the data for you. In order to parse the JSON data in this chapter, I will be using Python's built-in `json` module. As mentioned previously, the structure of Python dictionaries and arrays correspond to the structures of JSON data, so representing JSON data in Python is quite intuitive.

# Modules in Python

A Python **module** is a set of already made code that can be included in a program to add on extra functionality.

**Built-in modules** are modules that come with most Python installations. They are generally available without any additional installation or setup.

Other modules, called **external modules,** are built and maintained by businesses and by the open source community and can be installed separately. I will be using a few external modules in later chapters.

A module is included in a particular program using an `import` statement as follows:

```
import <name_of_module>
```

If the module is a built-in module (or an external module that has been installed properly), the `import` statement will load in all of the code for the named module. Otherwise, the statement will produce an error, because it will not be able to find the named module.

It is best practice to write `import` statements at the beginning of a program before any other code. Putting `import` statements at the beginning of your code helps yourself and others figure out what tools are required to run your code. Additionally, if your code attempts to use a module before it is imported, the program will produce an error. Putting `import` statements at the beginning of the program helps you avoid this mistake.

# Parsing a JSON file using the json module

The next step is to use `json` module to read and parse the data in the `scf_data.json` file. The following instructions describe how to use the `json` module:

1.  In the `process_data.py` file, open the `json` module using an `import` statement as follows. Not surprisingly, the name used to `import` the module is `json`.

    ```
    a built-in module or an import json

    inFile = open("data/input_data.json",'r')
    print(inFile.read())
    inFile.close()
    ```

2.  The `load()` function of the `json` module reads and parses the data in a JSON file. Use the `json.load()` function to load the contents of the `file` object and assign the result to a variable called `scf_data`. In the following continuation of , the `scf_data` variable contains the parsed data from the JSON file. Note that the call to `json.load()` should be placed between the opening and closing of the input file:

    ```
    import json

    inFile = open("data/input_data.json",'r')
    scf_data = json.load(inFile)
    print(inFile.read())
    inFile.close()
    ```

    The syntax used to call the `load` function of the json module (`'json.load()'`) is sometimes a bit confusing for beginners. This syntax has to do with a programming structure called **objects**. An object is a Python structure consisting of a collection of functions and variables. Objects are both a way of organizing code conceptually and of avoiding conflicts in variable and function names.

    In this book, I will not create any objects directly. However, functions and properties of objects will be used frequently, so it is helpful to be familiar with the syntax to use objects.

    In this case, `load()` is a function that belongs to the JSON object, which is created when the json module is imported. As the `load()` function belongs to the JSON object, the load is called by writing `json.load()`.

3. Next, instead of printing the raw data, print the `scf_data` variable containing the parsed JSON data as is done in the following continuation of `process_data.py`:

```
import json

inFile = open("data/input_data.json",'r')
scf_data = json.load(inFile)
print(scf_data)
inFile.close()
```

4. Go ahead and run the program. You should see the parsed JSON data printed to the output:

In the Terminal output, the appearance of the parsed data may not look that different from that of the raw data. However, the two are quite different. In the raw format, the data is simply represented as a Python string. In the parsed format, however, the data is represented as a collection of nested Python dictionaries and Python lists. This means that it is possible to manipulate the data programmatically.

# Exploring the contents of a data file

Before writing code to process a dataset, you first need to know some information about the contents of the dataset. This is slightly different from exploratory data analysis, in which the goal is to draw insight from the data.

The details of your initial exploration generally depend on what you already know about a particular dataset and what you ultimately intend to do with the data. That being said, there are a few questions that are usually helpful to ask:

- How is the data structured?
    - If the dataset is tabular, the answer to this question is rather simple. However, for a hierarchical dataset, there may be a relatively loose structure of the data.
- What are the data variables?
- For each available variable, what is the data type and what is the range of possible values?
- Are there any errors, missing values, or outliers in the data that can be corrected?

It is not always necessary to do this exploration programmatically. However, often files are too big or messy to look at in a regular text editor or in Excel.

# Extracting the core content of the data

The core content of a dataset is usually a series of data entries with identical properties. As mentioned previously, tabular data sources have a more predictable structure, so this step isn't really necessary for something like a CSV file.

Hierarchical data sources, on the other hand, will often include metadata with information about the dataset along with the data itself. There may also be variations in the structure of individual data entries, but for now all data entries will have the same variables.

Metadata can be useful, but in order to make use of the data, you will usually need to separate the core content of the dataset and put it in a more basic format. In the following steps, you will explore the structure of the data and find the core content:

1. As mentioned previously, in the Python representation of JSON data, every level of data is either a dictionary or a Python list. A good place to start is to see whether the data is a dictionary or a list at the base level. First, comment out the existing `print` function, as this is no longer needed. Next, use Python's built-in `type()` function to determine the type of data. Print out the result of the `type` function:

```
import json

######### OPEN AND READ THE DATA FILE ###########
inFile = open("data/input_data.json","r")
scf_data = json.load(inFile)
# print(scf_data)
inFile.close()

############ DATA EXPLORATION #############
dataType = str(type(scf_data))
print("type of data: " + dataType)
```

You should see an output that prints the type of the data inside angle brackets:

```
Terminal
allan@allan-ThinkPad-W510 ~/Documents/book/ch3/ch3 $ python3 process_data.py
type of data: <class 'dict'>
allan@allan-ThinkPad-W510 ~/Documents/book/ch3/ch3 $
```

Note that in the previous example, I combined (or **concatenated**) the print value with a description string. This is a useful technique to indicate which value is being printed. This is particularly useful when you have a lot of `print` functions in a particular program.

2. The data at the base level takes the form of a dictionary, so the next step is to see which keys are in the dictionary. This can tell you a bit about how the data is organized. You can use the `keys` function of the dictionary object in order to print out the dictionary keys:

```
############ DATA EXPLORATION #############
dataType = str(type(scf_data))
print("type of data: " + dataType)
```

```
print("dictionary keys: " + str(scf_data.keys()))
```

You should see three keys printed to the output: `metadata`, `issues`, and `errors`. The metadata key is rather self-explanatory; the corresponding value of the metadata key is information about the data rather than the data itself. In this case, the errors key refers to any errors that occurred in the process of retrieving the data. (This has to do with APIs, a topic I will discuss in detail in `Chapter 8`, *Getting Data from the Web*.)

3. As this dataset contains civic issue reports, it makes sense to assume that the `issues` key refers to the core data. To be sure, as shown in the following continuation of `process_data.py`, print out the type of the value of the `issues` key to see if it is a list:

```
. . .
print("dictionary keys: " + str(scf_data.keys()))
issues_data_type = str(type(scf_data["issues"]))
print("data type of the 'issues' value: " + issues_data_type )
```

You should see now that the value of the `issues1.` key is indeed a Python list:

```
Terminal
allan@allan-ThinkPad-W510 ~/Documents/book/ch3/ch3 $ python3 process_data.py
type of data: <class 'dict'>
dictionary keys: dict_keys(['errors', 'metadata', 'issues'])
data type of the 'issues' value: <class 'list'>
allan@allan-ThinkPad-W510 ~/Documents/book/ch3/ch3 $
```

4. Finding a list structure in a JSON dataset does not guarantee that it contains the core data; however, it is a good indication, particularly if it is a long list. To check whether the `issues` list contains the data, print out the first element of the list:

```
. . .
print("data type of the 'issues' value: " + issues_data_type )
print("first element of 'issues' list:")
print(scf_data["issues"][0])
```

The result that is printed is a Python dictionary with key value pairs for each data variable:

```
  ⊗ ● ◎   Terminal

allan@allan-ThinkPad-W510 ~/Documents/book/ch3/ch3 $ python3 process_data.py
type of data: <class 'dict'>
dictionary keys: dict_keys(['issues', 'metadata', 'errors'])
data type of the 'issues' value: <class 'list'>
first element of 'issues' list:
{'flag_url': 'https://seeclickfix.com/api/v2/issues/3662906/flag', 'status': 'Op
en', 'address': '467 Manila Ave Jersey City, NJ 07302, USA', 'point': {'coordina
tes': [-74.04202270507812, 40.726032257080008], 'type': 'Point'}, 'lng': -74.0420
227050781, 'created_at': '2017-08-26T18:06:52-04:00', 'comment_url': 'https://se
eclickfix.com/api/v2/issues/3662906/comments', 'id': 3662906, 'request_type': {'
title': 'Streets: Pothole/sinkhole/uneven pavement', 'related_issues_url': 'http
s://seeclickfix.com/api/v2/issues?lat=40.7260322570801&lng=-74.0420227050781&req
uest_types=11923&sort=distance', 'organization': 'City of Jersey City', 'url': '
https://seeclickfix.com/api/v2/request_types/11923', 'id': 11923}, 'url': 'https
://seeclickfix.com/api/v2/issues/3662906', 'html_url': 'https://seeclickfix.com/
issues/3662906', 'rating': 1, 'description': 'This one is DEEP, around six inche
```

This makes sense; it indicates that the `issues` list is a list of data entries represented by Python dictionaries. At this point, you've explored the structure of the dataset and found the core data.

> When working with future datasets, keep in mind that there is no one formula to navigate the structure of hierarchical data. Sometimes, the data source will offer documentation, and other times you may need to improvise.

Now that you have located the core content of the dataset, the next step is to take a look at some of the details. It is helpful if there is some documentation provided with a dataset to describe the names and types of variables in the dataset. Often however this is not the case.

In the next subsection, I will walk through some steps to display the contents of a data entry in an easy to read format. This will help you to observe what data variables are available and which variables might be of interest to you.

## Listing out all of the variables in the data

While working with a dataset, it is good practice to keep organized notes for your own reference. Within the `ch1` project folder, make a new subfolder called `notes`. In the notes subfolder, make a new file called `data_variables.txt`.

I'm going to use Python's built-in `pprint` (Pretty Print) module in order to show the data variables a bit more cleanly. The documentation for the `pprint` module is available at `https://docs.Python.org/3.6/library/pprint.html`.

The following continuation of `process_data.py` the first data entry is printed using the `pprint` module with a format that is easily readable:

```
...

# print(scf_data["issues"][0])

pp = pprint.PrettyPrinter(indent=4)
print("first data entry:")
pp.pprint(scf_data["issues"][0])
```

At this point, you can comment out all of the previous print functions from your initial exploration as these are no longer needed. After running the code in the previous example, you should see a *Pretty Printed* result:

```
● ● ●   Terminal
allan@allan-ThinkPad-W510 ~/Documents/book/ch3/ch3 $ python3 process_data.py
first data entry:
{    'acknowledged_at': None,
     'address': '467 Manila Ave Jersey City, NJ 07302, USA',
     'closed_at': None,
     'comment_url': 'https://seeclickfix.com/api/v2/issues/3662906/comments',
     'created_at': '2017-08-26T18:06:52-04:00',
     'description': 'This one is DEEP, around six inches, definitely a major '
                    'hazard needs repair immediately before people get '
                    'seriously hurt.',
     'flag_url': 'https://seeclickfix.com/api/v2/issues/3662906/flag',
     'html_url': 'https://seeclickfix.com/issues/3662906',
     'id': 3662906,
     'lat': 40.7260322570801,
     'lng': -74.0420227050781,
     'media': {    'image_full': 'https://seeclickfix.com/files/issue_images/0085/
7979/1503785141574.jpg',
                   'image_square_100x100': 'https://seeclickfix.com/files/issue_im
ages/0085/7979/1503785141574_square.jpg',
                   'representative_image_url': 'https://seeclickfix.com/files/issu
e_images/0085/7979/1503785141574_square.jpg',
                   'video_url': None},
     'point': {    'coordinates': [-74.04202270507812, 40.72603225708008],
                   'type': 'Point'},
     'rating': 1,
     'reopened_at': None,
     'request_type': {    'id': 11923,
                          'organization': 'City of Jersey City',
                          'related_issues_url': 'https://seeclickfix.com/api/v2/is
sues?lat=40.7260322570801&lng=-74.0420227050781&request_types=11923&sort=distanc
e',
                          'title': 'Streets: Pothole/sinkhole/uneven pavement',
                          'url': 'https://seeclickfix.com/api/v2/request_types/119
23'},
     'shortened_url': None,
     'status': 'Open',
     'summary': 'Streets: Pothole/sinkhole/uneven pavement',
     'transitions': {    'close_url': 'https://seeclickfix.com/api/v2/issues/36629
06/close'},
     'updated_at': '2017-08-26T18:06:54-04:00',
     'url': 'https://seeclickfix.com/api/v2/issues/3662906'}
allan@allan-ThinkPad-W510 ~/Documents/book/ch3/ch3 $
```

Go ahead and copy the result from your Terminal and paste it to your notes. Copying from and pasting to Terminals is sometimes a bit of a headache or not possible so you can alternatively take a screenshot.

At this point, you should be prepared to process the dataset and make some changes. In the next section, I will walk through some steps to extract certain data variables from the original dataset and create a new output with only the selected variables.

# Modifying a dataset

Looking over the data variables available in your notes, you should be able to get a sense of what information is available in each data entry and what information might be useful to you. Once you have observed the contents of a dataset, modification of the data is naturally what comes next. Here are some examples of changes that you might make:

- Extracting particular data variables
- Merging data sources
- Converting between formats
- Restructuring the data
- Removing outliers
- Correcting errors

In this exercise, I'm just going to extract some data variables from the original dataset, specifically the following:

- `address`
- `created_at`
- `description`
- `lng`
- `lat`
- `rating`

# Extracting data variables from the original dataset

In the following steps, you will iterate through the data entries of the original dataset using a for loop. For each of the individual entries, you will collect the previously mentioned variables into a new data entry and place the new data entries in to an array.

As is done in the following continuation of `process_data.py`, create an empty array called `new_scf_data`. This is the array where you will place the modified data entries. Copy the previously listed data variables into an array of strings called `variables`. These strings will be used as keys to access the values from the original data entries:

```
...
# pp.pprint(scf_data["issues"][0])

########### DATA MODIFICATION ############
new_scf_data = []
variables = ["address","created_at","description","lng","lat","rating"]
```

## Using a for loop to iterate over the data

Since data usually consists of a sequence of entries, the natural way to apply programmatic operations on each entry is to use a for loop.

After the `new_scf_data` array is created, create a for loop. The for loop should iterate over each of the data entries in the original dataset. In the body of the for loop, create a new Python dictionary called `new_entry`. The `new_entry` dictionary will contain the extracted variables from the entry of the original dataset. The following continuation of `process_data.py` demonstrates how this is done:

```
########### DATA MODIFICATION ############
new_scf_data = []
for old_entry in scf_data["issues"]:
    new_entry={}
```

## Using a nested for loop to iterate over the data variables

Each of the data variables should be extracted from the old entry and placed in the new entry. This can be done using a **nested for loop**, an additional for loop inside the base for loop. You can use a nested for loop to iterate over each of the data variables in the `variables` array.

Within the base for loop, create a new nested for loop that iterates over the elements in the `variables` array. In the nested for loop, write a statement that sets the value of each variable in the new array to the value of the variable in the old array:

```
...
for old_entry in issues:
    new_entry = {}
    for variable in variables:
```

```
new_entry[variable] = old_entry[variable]
```

It may be helpful to print out content at this point just to make sure that the loop is set up properly. This is optional, but if you would like to test the code, you can add a print function after the nested for loop to verify that each of the variables are added to the new data entry. This is demonstrated in the following continuation of `process_data.py`:

```
...
for old_entry in issues:
    new_entry = {}
    for variable in variables:
        new_entry[variable] = old_entry[variable]
    print(new_entry)
```

At this stage, with the `print` function from the previous example included, the following is the output on my system:

5. Finally, place each new entry into the `new_scf_data` array using the Python list `append()` method as follows:

```
...
for old_entry in issues:
    new_entry = {}
    for variable in variables:
        new_entry[variable] = old_entry[variable]
    # print(new_entry)
    new_scf_data.append(new_entry)
```

The `append` function is called by writing `.append()` directly after the name of a Python list as follows:
`<array_variable>.append(<value>)`
Calling the `append` function places the value that is passed in at the end of the array.

So far `process_data.py` creates a Python list containing the new data entries with the extracted data variables, however the new data disappears after the program is finished running. In order to preserve the data for future use, you will need to output a file containing the revised dataset. In the next section, I will walk through the steps for outputting data from python to a JSON file.

# Outputting the modified data to a new file

A new file can be created by opening a file with write permission. If named file does not exist, it will be created so long as the directory specified in the file path exists.

As is done in the following continuation of `process_data.py`, open a new output file in the `data` folder called `scf_output_data.json` with write permission.

In general, when you open a file with write permission, remember to be careful not to accidentally overwrite an existing file by using the name of a file you do not want to erase. Additionally remember to use double backslashes instead of forward slashes for file paths if you are using Windows

```
. . .
for issue in issues:
    new_issue = {}
    for variable in variables: ##
        new_issue[variable] = issue[variable] ##
    new_data.append(new_issue)

### OUTPUTTING THE NEW DATA TO A NEW FILE ###
outfile = open("data/scf_output_data.json","w")
outfile.close()
```

You can use the `json.dump()` method to write your data to the output file. The `json.dump()` method takes as arguments the `file` object for the output file as well as a Python dictionary or list to be written to the output file. In this case, I'm going to add the `indent` argument to the `json.dump()` function, which makes the result more human readable:

```
. . .
outfile = open("data/my_output_data.json","w")
json.dump(new_data, outfile, indent=4)
outfile.close()
```

Note that, in practice, the `pretty` option is only necessary if you intend to read the file in a text editor.

If the program works correctly, it should produce an output file called `scf_output_data.json` in the `data` folder. The output file should contain the new JSON data. As this particular output file isn't that big, you can open the file in Atom to verify that the output is correct:

# Specifying input and output file names in the Terminal

So far, you have specified the file names directly inside the program. Alternatively, it is possible to write your program so that you can specify the names of the input and output files in the Terminal when the program is run. This is particularly useful if you need to run the same program several times with different input datasets and collect several different output files.

The `sys` module allows you to access an array of strings that correspond to the parameters entered in the Terminal when a program is run. To get a sense for how this works, you can use create a basic program as follows to `import` the `sys` module and print out the parameter array:

```
import sys
print(sys.argv)
```

You can specify parameters to the program after the initial Python command separated by spaces, as follows:

```
$Python(3) json_code.py arg1 arg2 asdf fdsa
```

When running the preceding command, you will see that the parameters that you specified become the elements of the `argv` array that is printed out:

```
⊗◉◉  Terminal
allan@allan-ThinkPad-W510 ~/Documents/book/ch3/ch3 $ python
 sys_test.py arg1 arg2 asdf fdsa
['sys_test.py', 'arg1', 'arg2', 'asdf', 'fdsa']
allan@allan-ThinkPad-W510 ~/Documents/book/ch3/ch3 $
```

All that is needed now is to replace the names of the input and output files with elements from the `argv` array. In the following steps, I have copied the contents of `process_data.py` to a new program called `process_data2.py` which will be modified so that the input and output filenames can be specified in the terminal when the program is run.

# Specifying the filenames from the Terminal

1. Import the `sys` module:

   ```
   import json
   import sys

   inFile = open("data/input_data.json",'r')
   scf_data = json.load(inFile)
   ...
   ```

2. Change the input filename to `sys.argv[1]` and output filename to `sys.argv[2]`:

```
import json
import sys

inFile = open(sys.argv[1],'r')
scf_data = json.load(inFile)

. . .
. . .

outfile = open(sys.argv[2],"w")
json.dump(new_data, outfile, indent=4)
outfile.close()
```

3. Run the program followed by the input file and output file paths. This is for Windows:

```
$ python process_data.py data\\scf_data1.json
data\\scf_output_data2.json
```

This is for macOS and Linux:

```
$ python process_data.py data/scf_data1.json data/scf_output_data2.json
```

# Summary

This chapter was a basic overview of the steps involved in programmatically processing data files. To recap, I first introduced file I/O and demonstrated how the Python programming language interacts with the computer's filesystem. Then, I showed how a Python `file` object is used with the `json` module to read and parse a JSON files. Following this, I walked through a basic demonstration to show how you might go about exploring the contents of a data file. Once all of this was covered, I showed how to conduct some basic data modification steps. Finally, I showed how to write data to an output file.

A particular emphasis in this chapter was placed on the process of opening, parsing data and writing the result to the output. Using some frameworks like `R` and `Pandas` opening reading and writing files is more straight forward. Future chapters will focus more on the exploration and modification steps and much less on the specifics of inputting and outputting data. Understanding how to interact with files programmatically however is helpful when you need to be *specific* about the way data is opened, parsed or written.

The next chapter will a continuation and extension of the content in this chapter with additional opportunities to practice processing data in python. In the next chapter, I will extend the workflow developed in this chapter to CSV and XML, two additional file formats that are popular for the storing of data.

# 4
# Reading, Exploring, and Modifying Data - Part II

In the previous chapter, you learned how to apply Python programming to the task of processing data from external files. This chapter will build on the skills covered in the previous chapter with an introduction to the XML and CSV data formats. In addition to python's built-in tools for handling CSV and XML files, I will also cover pandas, which is a popular framework for working with tabular data. This chapter will include the following sections:

- Logistical overview
- Understanding the CSV format
- Introducing the `csv` module
- Using the `csv` module to read and process CSV data
- Using the `csv` module to write CSV data
- Using the `pandas` module to read and process data
- Handling non-standard CSV encoding and dialect
- Understanding XML
- Using the `xml.etree.ElementTree` module to parse XML data

## Logistical overview

In this chapter, I will demonstrate four projects, using four programs respectively. These are as follows:

- `csv_intro.py`: An introduction to Python's built-in `csv` module

- `pandas_intro.py`: An introduction to the `pandas` module
- `json_to_csv.py`: An exercise in working with CSV data
- `xml_to_json.py`: An introduction to the `xml.etree.ElementTree` module and an exercise in working with XML data

The finished product for each of these projects can be obtained from the code folder in the external resources. All of the external resources are available in one folder at the following link: `https://goo.gl/8S58ra`.

# File system setup

To follow along with the exercises, you should create a project folder called `ch4` to contain all of the code and data. There are a number of different programs, input datasets, and output datasets involved in the projects and exercises in this chapter. To keep things organized, I've created an additional folder to contain the code for the chapter. I've also fragmented the data folder to separate the input data from the output data. Lastly, I've created a folder to store my notes on the file structure and contents. The following is the file structure that I will be using:

```
ch4/
-->code/
---->csv_intro.py
---->pandas_intro.py
---->json_to_csv.py
---->xml_to_json.py
-->data/
---->input_data/
------>scf_extract.json
------>roads_by_country.csv
------>wikipedia.xml
---->output_data/
---->notes/
------>roads_by_country.txt
------>wikipedia.txt
```

If you use a different file structure, keep in mind that the file paths in your program may differ from those used in the book.

# Data

For this chapter, I will be using three datasets. The first of these, `scf_extract.json`, is the output from the `Chapter 3`, *Reading, Exploring, and Modifying Data - Part I*, exercise. The second, `artificial_roads_by_region.csv`, is a fabricated dataset containing the total road length of all of the roads in different made-up regions. The third dataset is an XML file containing the search results for Wikipedia articles about data wrangling. This data was obtained from the Wikipedia search API--details are provided along with the dataset. All datasets can be retrieved from the data folder in the external resources at `https://goo.gl/v4dLc3`. The data should be placed in the `data/input_data` folder of this chapter's project directory.

# Installing pandas

As mentioned previously, I will do a brief introduction to pandas in this chapter. Pandas is a popular framework for working with tabular data. To follow along with the demonstration, you will need to install the `pandas` module. I've included links to installation instructions in the *Installation* document in the external resources.

# Understanding the CSV format

**CSV**, which stands for **comma-separated value**, is a file format used to store tabular data. As you may have guessed, a CSV file consists of text values that are separated by commas.

In a CSV file, each data entry is represented by a single line. (Another way of thinking about this is that each line is separated by a newline `'\n'` character, though newline characters are invisible in most text editors.)

By convention, the first row in a CSV file contains the **column headers**, or the names attributed to each column. In each subsequent row, the position of each value corresponds to the data variable to which that value belongs. In other words, the first value in a row corresponds to the first column header, the second value in a row corresponds to the second column header, and so on. The following example demonstrates the syntax of a CSV file:

```
<header1>, <header2>, <header3>, <header4>, <header5>
<value1>, <value2>, <value3>, <value4>, <value5>
<value1>, <value2>, <value3>, <value4>, <value5>
<value1>, <value2>, <value3>, <value4>, <value5>
<value1>, <value2>, <value3>, <value4>, <value5>
```

You can think of the CSV format as the most basic version of a spreadsheet. In fact, most spreadsheet programs can open and edit CSV files. Of course, there are spreadsheet features (like formulas) that can't be represented in a CSV file. It is often useful, however, to process data that originates from a spreadsheet program like Excel. This can be done by saving or exporting in CSV format.

There are two ways to process CSV data in Python. The first of these is to use Python's built-in **CSV** module. The second is to use an external module called **pandas.** In the following exercises, I will introduce both methods as both may be handy depending on the use case.

# Introducing the CSV module

The `csv` module is designed to process CSV data in an iterative manner. Rather than reading the data and then processing it, the `csv` module is designed to simultaneously read and process the data line by line.

This makes sense from an efficiency perspective. It takes less memory and less time to read and operate on the data entry by entry than it does to read the data as whole. For this reason, the `csv` module is well suited to process very large data files that are too big to read into memory.

Additionally, because the `csv` module is built-in, it will work with any Python installation, making it transferable. This is worth mentioning because it is a slight advantage of the `csv` module over the `pandas` module.

In the following exercise, I will demonstrate how to use the `csv` module to read and process data.

# Using the CSV module to read CSV data

In this first demonstration, you will read the `artificial_roads_by_region.csv` file and get an estimate of the total length of roads as of 2011.

The first step to using the CSV module is to import the module, as shown in the following example:

```
import csv
```

The next step, similar to the process use in `Chapter 3`, *Reading, Exploring, and Modifying Data - Part I*, is to open the file containing the data. Recall that for this chapter, the code is one directory up from the base directory. This means that in the path to the data, you will first need to go back one directory using `../` in macOS and Linux or `..\\` in Windows. In the following demonstration, I've created a Python script called `csv_intro.py` in which the `open()` function is used to open `artificial_roads_by_region.csv` with read permission:

```
import csv

## open the file containing the data
fin =
open("../data/input_data/artificial_roads_by_region.csv","r",newline="")
```

 You may have noticed that a new parameter, `newline=""`, was added to the `open()` function. This reflects a best practice described in the documentation at `https://docs.python.org/3/library/csv.html#id3`.

In `Chapter 3`, *Reading, Exploring, and Modifying Data - Part I*, when reading in JSON data, the `json` module was used with the file object to read all of the data at once. Similarly, the `csv` module uses a file object to read data, but it does not read all of the data at once. Instead the `csv.DictReader()` function takes as a parameter a file object and returns a `reader` object which reads and parses CSV data line by line.

The following continuation of `csv_intro.py`, demonstrates how to create a reader object:

```
import csv

## open the file containing the data
fin =
open("../data/input_data/artificial_roads_by_region.csv","r",newline="")

## create a csv reader using the file object, 'fin'
reader = csv.DictReader(fin)
```

A CSV reader is what is called a **Python iterable**, which is an object that works like an array when used with a for loop. When using the `csv` module, a CSV file is read and parsed by iterating over the corresponding `reader` object using a for loop. This is done using a for loop as the following example demonstrates:

```
for row in <reader>:
    <do something with row...>
```

The `Dict` in the `DictReader` stands for dictionary. Behind the scenes, the `reader` object parses each line one by one into a Python dictionary, where the keys correspond to the column headers and the values correspond to the row values.

> The `csv` module also has a more basic reader that parses the data row by row into arrays, but the dictionary reader is more appropriate for this project.

To retrieve the column headers from the `reader` object, you can use the `reader.fieldnames` value. In the following continuation of `csv_intro.py`, the column headers of the CSV file are printed to the output:

```
....
reader = csv.DictReader(fin)

## print the column headers
print("column headers:")
print(reader.fieldnames)

fin.close()
```

When running `csv_intro.py`, you should see the column headers printed to the output as follows:

```
Terminal
allan@allan-ThinkPad-W510 ~/Documents/book/ch4/ch4/code $ python3 csv_intro.py
column headers:
['region name', '2011', '2010', '2009', '2008', '2007', '2006', '2005', '2004',
'2003', '2002', '2001', '2000']
allan@allan-ThinkPad-W510 ~/Documents/book/ch4/ch4/code $
```

Go ahead and copy the headers into your notes for the project. These can be used to access the individual fields from each row.

Next, you can create a for loop to read the data. A good first step when using the CSV module is to print out the first ten rows or so. This can help you identify the type of data in each column if it is not clear, and in particular, the way in which **NA values** (values that are missing or not available) are represented. In order to count the total road length in 2011, you will need to recognize and skip over NA values. In the following continuation of `csv_intro.py`, the `reader.line_num` property is used to check the line number and print the first 10 lines:

```
....
print(reader.fieldnames)

total_roads=0
## iterate over the rows in the CSV file
print("first 10 values of the 2011 column:")
for row in reader:
    ## print out the first 10 values of 2011
    if reader.line_num <= 11:
        print(row["2011"])

fin.close()
```

At this stage, running `csv_intro.py` should produce the following output:

```
allan@allan-ThinkPad-W510 ~/Documents/book/ch4/ch4/code $ python3 csv_intro.py
column headers:
['region name', '2011', '2010', '2009', '2008', '2007', '2006', '2005', '2004',
'2003', '2002', '2001', '2000']
first 10 values of the 2011 column:

1136.9180229386748

1415.1812352929992
4054.432799406344
752.2232420096623

829.2274043984817
1066.0017235125226
1390.2547000255238
allan@allan-ThinkPad-W510 ~/Documents/book/ch4/ch4/code $
```

There are two things to notice from the output. First, the numbers are formatted as strings with trailing decimal points. It is not clear from the output that the numbers are strings, though numbers are always encoded as character sequences in CSV files. You could verify this by printing the data type instead of the value using `type(row["2011"])`. You will need to convert the number strings to float types in Python in order to add the values.

The second thing to notice is that the NA values take the form of empty strings. This means that when adding values, empty strings, which represent NA values should be skipped.

After creating a loop to read and parse CSV data, one possible (though not so elegant) approach to processing the data is to create a nested array to store the data, as follows:

```
myData = [[<value1>],[<value2>],[<value3>],
    [<value1>],[<value2>],[<value3>],
    [<value1>],[<value2>],[<value3>],
    ....
]
```

This can work, but it doesn't take advantage of the efficiency of the CSV module. It is usually better to do any analysis or processing inside the loop used to read the data. This makes the code simpler and more efficient.

The goal of this project is to count up the total roads length as of 2011. As many of the data entries are missing, this will be a very rough estimate. In Chapter 6, *Cleaning Numerical Data - An Introduction to R and Rstudio*, I will show how to use R to clean numerical data and get a slightly better estimate. For now, this will be done by simply adding all of the values that are available.

In the following continuation of `csv_intro.py`, a variable called `total_roads` is created. In each iteration of the for loop introduced in previous steps, the `2011` value of each row is first checked to see if it is an empty string (if it is an NA value). If the value is not an empty string, it is converted from a `string` data type to a `float` data type and then added to `total_roads` variable. In this way, the total length of road is aggregated across all of the regions.

```
....
print(reader.fieldnames)

total_roads=0
## iterate over the rows in the CSV file
print("first 10 values of the 2011 column:")
for row in reader:
    ## print out the first 10 values of 2011
```

```
    if reader.line_num <= 11:
        print(row["2011"])
    if row["2011"] != "":
        total_roads+=float(row["2011"])

print("total length of roads as of 2011:")
print(total_roads)

fin.close()
```

At this stage, running `csv_intro.py` should produce the following output:

```
●●● Terminal
allan@allan-ThinkPad-W510 ~/Documents/book/ch4/ch4/code $ python3 csv_intro.py
column headers:
['region name', '2011', '2010', '2009', '2008', '2007', '2006', '2005', '2004',
'2003', '2002', '2001', '2000']
first 10 values of the 2011 column:

1136.9180229386748

1415.1812352929992
4054.432799406344
752.2232420096623

829.2274043984817
1066.0017235125226
1390.2547000255238
total leangth of roads as of 2011:
289176.99251196673
allan@allan-ThinkPad-W510 ~/Documents/book/ch4/ch4/code $
```

This demonstrates the process for using the `csv` module to read data. In the next section, I will demonstrate how to use the `csv` module to write data to a `csv` file.

# Using the CSV module to write CSV data

In this next demonstration, you will read the output data from the previous chapter and convert it to CSV format.

To start off with, I will create a file called `json_to_csv.py` which will make use of both the csv module and the json module. In the `json_to_csv.py` file, I will start by importing both the csv module and the json module and reading the JSON data from the `scf_extract.json` file into a Python list:

```
import csv
import json

## read in the input json data
fin = open("../data/input_data/scf_extract.json","r")
json_data = json.load(fin)
fin.close()
```

Writing CSV data using the csv module is a bit like reading data with the CSV module in reverse. When opening a file with write permission, you can use the corresponding file object to create a `writer` object. This is done using the `csv.writer()` function. The `writerow()` function of the `writer` object will take an array of values and write it to a row in the output file.

Recall that the extracted data entries from the previous chapter took the form of an array of dictionaries. To demonstrate this visually, the following is the structure of the data:

```
[
    {<key1>:<value1>,<key2>,<value2>,...},
    {<key1>:<value1>,<key2>,<value2>,...}
    {<key1>:<value1>,<key2>,<value2>,...}
    ...
]
```

Converting `scf_extract.py` to CSV format will involve changing each data entry into a Python list, where the values are in a fixed order. Python dictionaries and JSON key value pairs are not necessarily in a fixed order. In order to keep the values in a fixed order that corresponds to the column headers, the approach used here will be to create an array of the column headers. For each data entry, the array of column headers can be used to extract each value in order and place it in an array of values.

First, in the following continuation of `csv_to_json.py`, the keys of the first data entry (which correspond to the data variables in the dataset) are placed into a Python list. This Python list will be used as the reference of the column headers of the output file:

```
....
json_data = json.load(fin)
fin.close()

## get an array of data variables to
```

```
## use as column headers
keys = json_data[0].keys()
```

Next, an output file is opened with write permission and the corresponding file object is used to create a `writer` object. The `writer.writerow()` function is used to write the first row (containing the column headers) to the output file:

```
....
keys = json_data[0].keys()

## open an output file with write permission
## and create a writer object
fout = open("../data/output_data/scf_extract.csv","w")
writer = csv.writer(fout)
writer.writerow(keys)

fout.close()
```

The last step will be to iterate over each of the entries in the `json_data` variable. Each data entry from the original dataset should be converted from dictionary to a Python list, and written to the output CSV file.

In the following continuation of `json_to_csv.py`, a for loop is created to iterate over the entries in the JSON dataset. In a nested for loop, each of the data variables are extracted one by one and placed in a fixed order into a Python list. The resulting Python list is then written to a row in the output CSV file:

```
....
writer.writerow(keys)

## iterate over the json data extracting
## the data variables into an ordered list
## write each data entry to the output file
for entry in json_data:
    row=[]
    for key in keys:
        row.append(entry[key])
    writer.writerow(row)

fout.close()
```

That's it for the CSV module! If you are interested in learning more, I've made a link to the documentation for the `csv` module available in the Links and Further Reading document of the external resources.

The next section will be an introduction to the `pandas` module which uses a different approach for processing tabular data. In the next section, I will revisit the task of counting the total road length as of 2011 in order to demonstrate some of the differences.

# Using the pandas module to read and process data

Pandas is a set of tools for easy manipulation and analysis of tabular data. Among these tools is an object for representing and manipulating tabular data called a **dataframe**. With a dataframe, it is possible to express row-wise and column-wise operations to be performed on the data. Pandas can simplify the process of working with data considerably, requiring fewer lines of code and making the process more intuitive.

## Counting the total road length in 2011 revisited

In this next demonstration, you will approach the same problem of enumerating the road length--this time using pandas. To start off with, create a file called `pandas_intro.py` that import the `pandas` module as follows:

```
import pandas
```

Reading CSV data using the `pandas` module is quite simple. Pandas combines the process of opening a file with the process of reading and parsing the data. To read a CSV file using the `pandas` module, you can use the `pandas.read_csv()` function. The `pandas.read_csv()` function takes as input the path to a file and returns a pandas dataframe. In the following continuation of `pandas_intro.py`, the `pandas.read_csv()` function is used to read the data from `artificial_roads_by_region.csv` into a pandas dataframe called `roads_by_country`:

```
import pandas

## read the csv file into a pandas dataframe
roads =
pandas.read_csv("../data/input_data/artificial_roads_by_region.csv")
```

In the next step, I will add a couple lines to `pandas_intro.py` to print the column headers of the dataframe using the Python `list()` function. The `list()` function converts an item to a Python list. When used with a pandas dataframe, the `list()` function returns a Python list with the column headers of the dataframe.

```
import pandas

## read the csv file into a pandas dataframe
roads =
pandas.read_csv("../data/input_data/artificial_roads_by_region.csv")

## print out the column headers
print("column headers:")
print(list(roads))
```

In pandas, columns can be indexed using the column names, similar to the way dictionaries are indexed using keys. In the following continuation of `pandas_intro.py`, the `2011` column is selected from the dataframe and printed. An individual column selected from pandas dataframe is a slightly different object called a pandas **series** that functions similarly to a dataframe:

```
. . . .
# print(list(roads))

## extract roads from 2011
roads_2011 = roads['2011']
print(roads_2011)
```

Printing a pandas dataframe or series just prints the beginning and end of each column so that it won't flood your terminal. The following is the output on my machine from running `pandas_intro.py` as this stage:

```
979           NaN
980           NaN
981           NaN
982    1112.575897
983           NaN
984           NaN
985           NaN
986    1184.276882
987     757.897789
988    1212.507237
989           NaN
990     991.782095
991           NaN
992           NaN
993    1137.327405
994           NaN
995           NaN
996           NaN
997           NaN
998    1034.365895
999           NaN
Name: 2011, Length: 1000, dtype: float64
allan@allan-ThinkPad-W510 ~/Documents/book/ch4/ch4/code $
```

You may have noticed that several of the values printed to the output are of the type NA. This is because pandas automatically detects an empty string and assigns its own datatype for an NA value. You do not need to remove NA values for this project as pandas will simply skip over them automatically.

Converting between datatypes in pandas can be done using the `dataframe.astype()` or `series.as_type()` function. The functions take as input a string that indicates the data type to be converted to. Recall that in the previous exercise the 2011 column was originally a string datatype, and needed to be converted to a float datatype. In the following continuation of `pandas_intro.py`, the values of the `roads_2011` series are converted from a string data type to a float data type:

```
# print(roads_2011)

## convert the data type from string to float
roads_2011_2 = roads_2011.astype('float')
```

Once the data is converted, the last step is to add all of the values in the `roads_2011_2` column. The `dataframe.sum()` function, of the `series.sum()` function can be used to add the values of a pandas `dataframe` or pandas `series` respectively. Both skip over NA values automatically. In the following continuation of `pandas_intro.py`, the sum of the values in the 2011 column is calculated:

```
. . . .
roads_2011_2 = roads_2011.astype('float')

## find the sum of the values from 2011
total_2011 = roads_2011_2.sum()

print("total length of roads as of 2011:")
print(total_2011)
```

At this stage, running `pandas_intro.csv` should produce the following output:

Pandas also makes it possible to select multiple columns at once using an array of column names. In the following continuation of `pandas_intro.py`, a new dataframe is created that just contains every column except for the non-numerical column with the region name:

```
....
# print(total_2011)

## create a list of columns to extract
columns =
["2011","2010","2009","2008","2007","2006","2005","2004","2003","2002","200
1","2000"]
## extract the numerical data variables
roads_num = roads[columns]
```

Alternatively, the previous step could be expressed more concisely, using the `dataframe.drop()` function, which drops a particular set of columns or rows. Here is a more concise way of removing the `region name` column:

```
## the more concise way
roads_num = roads.drop("region name",axis=1)
```

Finally, the `dataframe.sum()` function can be used to add multiple columns at once. In the following continuation of `pandas_intro.py`, the total for every year is found simultaneously.

```
. . . . .
roads_num = roads.drop("region name",axis=1)

# ## sum along the vertical axis for all columns
total_by_year=roads_num.sum(0)

print("total road length by year:")
print(total_by_year)
```

Note that a parameter was passed to the `dataframe.sum()` function in order to specify that the sum should take place along the vertical axis.

Running `pandas_intro.py` at this point should print out a series of summed columns:

```
allan@allan-ThinkPad-W510 ~/Documents/book/ch4/ch4/code $ python pandas_intro.py
total road leangth by year:
2011    289176.992512
2010    300132.069320
2009    268843.441076
2008    302402.881170
2007    260148.339498
2006    254681.722026
2005    306296.389419
2004    289729.750629
2003    276180.510911
2002    289137.110303
2001    274696.000000
2000    288210.432498
dtype: float64
allan@allan-ThinkPad-W510 ~/Documents/book/ch4/ch4/code $
```

That's it for pandas! The way the `pandas` module works in Python is a bit analogous to the way tabular data is represented and processed in R. This will become clearer when I introduce R in Chapter 6, *Cleaning Numerical Data - An Introduction to R and Rstudio*. Because much of the functionality of the `pandas` module is similar to R, I have just done a brief coverage here. For more on pandas, I've made a link to the pandas documentation available in the Links and Further Reading document of the external resources.

# Handling non-standard CSV encoding and dialect

Most CSV data now is encoded using the standard Unicode formats that are used by default in Python. Occasionally however, you may come across a data file with an older or more obscure encoding format. In order to properly read and process data with a non-standard encoding, you will need to specify the encoding in the call to `open()` function that creates the file object. The `pandas.read_csv()` function also allows for the specification of non-standard encoding. I've made a link to the encoding formats accepted by Python in the *Links and Further Reading* document in the external resources.

There also may be variations in the **delimiter**, the character used to separate values, the **newline character** used to indicate the end of a line, and a few other formatting attributes. These variations are collectively referred to as the CSV **dialect**. Both the `pandas.read_csv()` function and the `csv.reader()` have parameters that allow you to specify variations in the formatting attributes of the CSV file you are reading from or writing to. I've made links to the documentation for both available in the *Links and Further Reading* document of the external resources.

# Understanding XML

XML, like JSON, is a hierarchical data format that allows a nested data structure. If you have worked with HTML before, you might be familiar with the general structure and syntax of XML, which HTML is based on.

An XML dataset consists of a nested *tree* of **elements** where each element may contain text with a particular value, another element or a collection of additional elements. Each element in the tree may also contain any number of **attributes** which describe the element.

Each element is represented by an **opening tag** and a **closing tag**. An opening tag indicates the beginning of an XML element. It is written by writing the name of the tag inside angle brackets. The following is what an XML opening tag looks like:

```
<tagname>
```

A closing tag follows the opening tag and indicates the end of an element. It is written by specifying the name of a tag inside angle brackets with a / before the name. The following is what an XML closing tag looks like:

```
</tagname>
```

In other parts of the book, angle brackets are used as a placeholder for some value or parameter. In the previous examples, and when displaying XML in general, the angle brackets are meant literally, as they are a part of the XML syntax.

The attributes of an element are written inside the opening tag. An attribute is specified with the attribute name follow by an = symbol followed by the value of the attribute inside " characters. The following is what the opening tag of an element with attributes looks like:

```
<tagname attribute1="value1" attribute2="value2">
```

Finally, the nested elements within an XML element are written between the opening and closing tags of the parent element. To make this human readable, the nested elements are typically written on separate lines with additional levels of indentation.

The following is an example of what a typical XML document might look like:

```
<XMLdocument>
    <metadata>
        <timecreated>
            5:00 AM
        </timecreated>
    </metadata>
    <dataformats>
        <dataformat type='hierarchical'>
            JSON
        </dataformat>
        <dataformat type='hierarchical'>
            XML
        </dataformat>
        <dataformat type='tabular'>
            CSV
        </dataformat>
    <dataformats>
</XMLdocument>
```

# XML versus JSON

XML and JSON can both be used for representing hierarchical data; however, JSON has become increasingly popular as a means of storing and distributing data. A big reason for this is that JSON is more compatible with JavaScript, a programming language critical for web development. That said, a number of current and legacy data sources are available only in XML, so it can be useful to know how to work with XML.

In the following section, I will do a brief introduction of the Python `xml.etree.ElementTree` module which can be used to process XML data.

# Using the XML module to parse XML data

In this next section, I will walk through some of the steps for using Python to parse and process XML data in a basic project to convert a dataset from XML to JSON.

In Python, XML is represented using a tree-like structure and parsed using the `xml.etree.ElementTree` module. Navigating this tree is a bit more sophisticated than navigating the structure of JSON data because the structure of XML does not fit as neatly into python data structures.

The first step to processing XML data is to read the XML data into Python's tree-like XML representation with the `xml.etree.ElementTree` module, using the following steps:

1. Import the `xml.etree.ElementTree` module.
2. Open the file containing the XML data.
3. Use the `ElementTree.parse()` function to create an `ElementTree` object.
4. Use the `.getroot` function of the `ElementTree` object to return an element object representing the root of the element tree.

The result is a representation of the XML data in python that you can navigate starting with the **root element**, or the element at the base of the XML tree. In the following demonstration, I've created a Python script called `xml_to_json.py`, which opens the XML dataset for this chapter, parses the data, and navigates to the root element:

```
import json
from xml.etree import ElementTree

fin = open("../data/input_data/wikipedia.xml","r")
tree = ElementTree.parse(fin)
root = tree.getroot()

fin.close()
```

The `root` variable at the end of the previous example is an **element object.** Specifically, it is the element object representing the element at the base of the tree.

An `element` object is Python's representation of an XML element, similar to the way a dictionaries and Python lists are Python's representation of JSON structures. With `element` objects, it is possible to navigate the XML tree by accessing a particular element's attributes, internal text, or child elements.

Once you have obtained an `element` object that represents the root element, the next step is to navigate from the document root to the part of the XML that contains the data you are looking for. As with JSON data, XML data sources often have good documentation to describe the structure and contents of a dataset. However, if documentation is not available for a particular dataset, it may be helpful to conduct a quick exploration of the dataset in order to find how the data is structured.

The `element.getchildren()` function of the `element` object can be used to retrieve an array of `element` objects that are the child elements of a particular element. In the the next few steps, I will continuously use `element.getchildren()` to search through the XML and display the contents of the XML data at various levels. This exploration will be similar to the exploration used in the previous chapter to navigate JSON data. The goal is to find the core content of the dataset within all of the metadata.

In the following continuation of `xml_to_json.py`, the `element.getchildren()` function is used to retrieve the child elements of the root element. The child elements are then printed to the output:

```
....
root = tree.getroot()

## search through the element tree
## for a long list of elements
data = root.getchildren()
print(data)

fin.close()
```

Running `xml_to_json.csv` at this stage should produce the following output:

```
● ● ●  Terminal
allan@allan-ThinkPad-W510 ~/Documents/book/ch4/ch4/code $ python3 xml_to_json.py

[<Element 'continue' at 0x7fe5fb1b2f98>, <Element 'query' at 0x7fe5fb1cf868>]
allan@allan-ThinkPad-W510 ~/Documents/book/ch4/ch4/code $
```

In the printout, it is possible to see the tag name of each element in the list of child elements. It is possible to expand to one of the child elements by selecting it's index from the Python list of child elements. The result is an `element` object representing the selected child element. The following demonstrates how you might expand to the child elements of the second child element of the root element:

```
data = root.getchildren()[1].getchildren()
```

This can be a rather primitive but effective way of navigating the contents of an XML file if the file is too big to open in a text editor.

After a few iterations of searching through the children, the following continuation of `xml_to_json.py` produces a relatively long list of elements that likely contain the relevant data:

```
. . . .

## search through the element tree
## for a long list of elements

data = root.getchildren()[1].getchildren()[1].getchildren()
print(data)

fin.close()
```

At this stage, running `xml_to_json.csv` should print out a list of element objects as follows:

There are two more features of `element` objects which can be useful in navigating and parsing XML data. The first is the `element.tag` value of an `element` object, which is a string containing the tag of the element. The second is the `element.attrib` value of an `element` object, which is a dictionary in which the keys correspond to the attribute names and the values correspond to the attribute values.

At this stage of `xml_to_json.py`, the `data` variable contains a list of `element` objects corresponding to a list of data entries in the XML data. In the following continuation of `xml_to_json.py`, the tag name and attributes of the first element are printed to the output.

```
....
data = root.getchildren()[1].getchildren()[1].getchildren()
# print(data)
print("item_tag:")
print(data[0].tag)
print("item_attributes:")
print(data[0].attrib)

fin.close()
```

Running `xml_to_json.py` at this stage shows that the `.attrib` value of each element is a dictionary in which the keys correspond to the data variables and the dictionary values correspond to the data values. This means converting to JSON will just involve retrieving the `.attrib` value of each element and placing the result into an array. The resulting array can be written to an output JSON file using the `json` module.

In the following continuation of `xml_to_json.py`, an array called `json_data` is created. A for loop iterates over each of the `element` objects and retrieves the `.attrib` value of each placing each of the resulting dictionaries in the `json_data` array. The `json_data` array is then written to a JSON file called `wikipedia.json`.

```
....
# print(data[0].attrib)

## iterate over the xml data converting
## each entry to json format
json_data=[]
for entry in data:
    json_data.append(entry.attrib)

## output the new data to a json file
fout = open("../data/output_data/wikipedia.json","w")
json.dump(json_data,fout,indent=4)

fin.close()
fout.close()
```

Running `xml_to_json.csv` should now produce a JSON version of the data in the `output_data` folder!

This has been a basic introduction to working with XML data. To read more about the `xml.etree.ElementTree` module and working with XML in Python, I have made a link available in the *Links and Further Reading* document in the external resources.

# XPath

*XPath* is a language for efficiently searching through and navigating XML data, which may be useful for some projects that require heavy use of XML data. XPath makes it possible to select elements in an XML tree using path-like expressions. The Python `xml.etree.ElementTree` module includes partial support for XPath.

I won't cover XPath in this book, but I've included some links to useful resources on XPath in the *Links and Further Reading* document in the external resources.

# Summary

In summary this chapter was an introduction to the XML and CSV data formats. In Python, CSV data can be processed using the Python `csv` module or using the `pandas` module depending on personal preference and the nature of the task. The `csv` module can also be used to write output CSV data. (While it was not covered here, it is also possible to use the pandas module to output data in CSV and JSON formats.) Finally, XML data can be parsed using the Python `xml.etree.ElementTree` module.

In the next chapter, you will have the chance to work on a much more applied project-- extracting street names from addresses. In the next chapter, I will introduce **regular expressions**, a tool for matching and extracting patterns in text data.

# 5
# Manipulating Text Data - An Introduction to Regular Expressions

Previous chapters have dealt with data manipulation of data on a *macroscopic* level, without much emphasis on the values in each data entry. In other words, the content up until this point has focused with processing datasets as a *whole*.

In these next two chapters, I will discuss data wrangling on a more *microscopic* level, placing emphasis on the individual values of the dataset. This chapter will be about working with text data. In this chapter, I will introduce and discuss the use of **regular expressions** to recognize patterns in strings. After a brief introduction of regular expressions, I will demonstrate a specific application of regular expressions in a project to extract street names from a dataset containing addresses.

This chapter will include the following sections:

- Logistical overview
- Understanding the need for pattern recognition
- Introducing regular expressions
- Looking for patterns
- Quantifying the existence of patterns
- Extracting patterns

# Logistical overview

Three Python scripts will be used for the demonstrations in this chapter. The first of these scripts, `regex_intro.py`, will be a program to introduce and demonstrate the use of regular expressions in Python. The second, `explore_addresses.py`, will be a simple program to explore the dataset and look for patterns. The third, `extract_street_names.py`, will be a program to extract the street names from the original dataset and output a revised dataset with a column for street names. The finished product for each of these files is available in the *code* folder of the reference material. All of the reference material can be found at the following link: `https://goo.gl/8S58ra`.

# Data

For the exercise in this chapter, you will be working with another dataset containing **Seeclickfix** issue reports. This time, I've put the dataset in the CSV format and extracted just a few fields from the data. I've also limited the entries to the continental US in order to make the address formats a bit more consistent.

The dataset used with this chapter, called `scf_adress_data.csv`, is available in the *data* document of the external resources.

# File structure setup

For this chapter, you should create a project folder called `ch5` that contains the code for the chapter. There should be a `data` folder in the project folder to contain the data for the chapter. You may copy and paste the data from the source into the data file:

```
ch5/
regex_intro.py
explore_addresses.py
extract_street_names.py
--data/
----scf_address_data.csv
```

# Understanding the need for pattern recognition

The simplest way to process the values of text fields to treat them as **categorical** variables. In a categorical variable, the data entries take on a fixed number of values. To illustrate working with categorical variables, consider a categorical field, such as the US states. If the state of Connecticut, for instance, were to appear in a large enough number of data entries, you might expect to see certain characteristic misspellings, such as the following:

- Conecticut
- Conneticut
- Connetict

An easy way to fix all of the misspellings might be to iterate through each of the data entries and check against a list of common misspellings as is done in the following demonstration. Note that the following code sample is just for demonstration purposes and doesn't belong to a particular file:

```
misspellings = ["Conecticut", "Conneticut", "Connectict"]
for ind in range(len(data)):
    if data[ind]["state"] in misspellings:
        data[ind]["state"] = "Connecticut
```

In the previous demonstration, incorrect text fields are corrected based on their exact value. It is often the case, however, that you will need to analyze and change text fields on a more structural level. Working with addresses is a good example of such a task. No two addresses are alike, but addresses generally fall under a certain structure.

Specifically, in the US, proper addresses are written as follows:

```
<house number> <street name> <city>, <state> <zipcode>
```
Text fields that contain structured information, such as addresses, are, in a way, like their own data type. Such text fields are represented in Python on an atomic level as a single string, but they may contain several pieces of information. Working with text fields such as addresses requires a new programming tool called **regular expressions**, which can search for patterns within strings.

# Introducting regular expressions

A **regular expression**, or **regex** for short, is simply a sequence of characters that specifies a certain search pattern. Regular expressions have been around for quite a while and are a field of computer science in and of themselves.

In Python, regular expression operations are handled using Python's built in `re` module. In this section, I will walk through the basics of creating regular expressions and using them to  You can implement a regular expression with the following steps:

1. Specify a **pattern string**.
2. Compile the pattern string to a `regular expression` object.
3. Use the `regular expression` object to search a string for the pattern.
4. Optional: Extract the matched pattern from the string.

# Writing and using a regular expression

The first step to creating a regular expression in Python is to import the `re` module:

```
import re
```

Python regular expressions are expressed using pattern strings, which are strings that specify the desired search pattern. In its simplest form, a pattern string can consist only of letters, numbers, and spaces. The following pattern string expresses a search query for an exact sequence of characters. You can think of each character as an individual pattern. In later examples, I will discuss more sophisticated patterns:

```
import re

pattern_string = "this is the pattern"
```

The next step is to process the pattern string into an object that Python can use in order to search for the pattern. This is done using the `compile()` method of the `re` module. The `compile()` method takes the pattern string as an argument and returns a `regex` object:

```
import re

pattern_string = "this is the pattern"
regex = re.compile(pattern_string)
```

Once you have a `regex` object, you can use it to search within a **search string** for the pattern specified in the pattern string. A search string is just the name for the string in which you are looking for a pattern. To search for the pattern, you can use the `search()` method of the `regex` object as follows:

```
import re

pattern_string = "this is the pattern"
regex = re.compile(pattern_string)
match = regex.search("this is the pattern")
```

If the pattern specified in the pattern string is in the search string, the `search()` method will return a `match` object. Otherwise, it returns the `None` data type, which is an empty value.

Since Python interprets `True` and `False` values rather loosely, the result of the `search` function can be used like a Boolean value in an `if` statement, which can be rather convenient:

```
....
match = regex.search("this is the pattern")
if match:
    print("this was a match!")
```

The search string *this is the pattern* should produce a match, because it matches exactly the pattern specified in the pattern string. The search function will produce a match if the pattern is found at any point in the search string as the following demonstrates:

```
....
match = regex.search("this is the pattern")
if match:
    print("this was a match!")
if regex.search("*** this is the pattern ***"):
    print("this was not a match!")
if not regex.search("this is not the pattern"):
    print("this was not a match!")
```

# Special characters

Regular expressions depend on the use of certain **special characters** in order to express patterns. Due to this, the following characters should not be used directly unless they are used for their intended purpose:

```
. ^ $ * + ? {} () [] | \
```

If you do need to use any of the previously mentioned characters in a pattern string to search for that character, you can write the character preceded by a backslash \ character. This is called **escaping** characters. Here's an example:

```
pattern string = "c\*b"
## matches "c*b"
```

If you need to search for the backslash character itself, you use two backslash characters, as follows:

```
pattern string = "c\\b"
## matches "c\b"
```

# Matching whitespace

Using \s at any point in the pattern string matches a whitespace character. This is more general then the space character, as it applies to tabs and newline characters:

```
. . . .
a_space_b = re.compile("a\sb")
if a_space_b.search("a b"):
    print("'a b' is a match!")
if a_space_b.search("1234 a b 1234"):
    print("'1234 a b 1234' is a match")
if a_space_b.search("ab"):
    print("'1234 a b 1234' is a match")
```

# Matching the start of string

If the ^ character is used at the beginning of the pattern string, the regular expression will only produce a match if the pattern is found at the beginning of the search string:

```
. . . .
a_at_start = re.compile("^a")
if a_at_start.search("a"):
    print("'a' is a match")
if a_at_start.search("a 1234"):
    print("'a 1234' is a match")
if a_at_start.search("1234 a"):
    print("'1234 a' is a match")
```

# Matching the end of a string

Similarly, if the $ symbol is used at the end of the pattern string, the regular expression will only produce a match if the pattern appears at the end of the search string:

```
....
a_at_end = re.compile("a$")
if a_at_end.search("a"):
    print("'a' is a match")
if a_at_end.search("a 1234"):
    print("'a 1234' is a match")
if a_at_end.search("1234 a"):
    print("'1234 a' is a match")
```

# Matching a range of characters

It is possible to match a range of characters instead of just one. This can add some flexibility to the pattern:

- [A-Z] matches all capital letters
- [a-z] matches all lowercase letters
- [0-9] matches all digits

```
....
lower_case_letter = re.compile("[a-z]")
if lower_case_letter.search("a"):
    print("'a' is a match")
if lower_case_letter.search("B"):
    print("'B' is a match")
if lower_case_letter.search("123 A B 2"):
    print("'123 A B 2' is a match")

digit = re.compile("[0-9]")
if digit.search("1"):
    print("'a' is a match")
if digit.search("342"):
    print("'a' is a match")
if digit.search("asdf abcd"):
    print("'a' is a match")
```

# Matching any one of several patterns

If there is a fixed number of patterns that would constitute a match, they can be combined using the following syntax:

```
(<pattern1>|<pattern2>|<pattern3>)
```

The following `a_or_b` regular expression will match any string where there is either an a character or a b character:

```
....
a_or_b = re.compile("(a|b)")
if a_or_b.search("a"):
    print("'a' is a match")
if a_or_b.search("b"):
    print("'b' is a match")
if a_or_b.search("c"):
    print("'c' is a match")
```

# Matching a sequence instead of just one character

If the + character comes after another character or pattern, the regular expression will match an arbitrarily long sequence of that pattern. This is quite useful, because it makes it easy to express something like a word or number that can be of arbitrary length.

# Putting patterns together

More sophisticated patterns can be produced by combining pattern strings one after the other. In the following example, I've created a regular expression that searches for a number strictly followed by a word. The pattern string that generates the regular expression is composed of the following:

- A pattern string that matches a sequence of digits: `[0-9]+`
- A pattern string that matches a whitespace character: `\s`
- A pattern string that matches a sequence of letters: `[a-z]+`
- A pattern string that matches either the end of the string or a whitespace character: `(\s|$)`

```
....
number_then_word = re.compile("[0-9]+\s[a-z]+(\s|$)")
```

```
if number_then_word.search("1234 asdf"):
    print("'1234 asdf' is a match")
if number_then_word.search("asdf 1234"):
    print("'asdf 1234' is a match")
if number_then_word.search("1234 1234"):
    print("'1234 1234' is a match")
```

# Extracting a pattern from a string

Recall that the `search()` method returns a `match` object if it locates the pattern in the search string. If you save the match object to a variable, you can use the `group()` function of the match object to retrieve the first occurrence of the pattern in the search string:

```
....
match = number_then_word.search("**** 1234 abcd ****")
print(match.group())
```

# The regex split() function

**Regex** objects in Python also have a `split()` method. The split method *splits* the search string into an array of substrings. The *splits* occur at each location along the string where the pattern is identified. The result is an array of strings that occur between instances of the pattern. If the pattern occurs at the beginning or end of the search string, an empty string is included at the beginning or end of the resulting array, respectively:

```
....
print(a_or_b.split("123a456b789"))
print(a_or_b.split("a1b"))
```

# Python regex documentation

If you are interested, the Python documentation has a more complete coverage of regular expressions. It can be found at `https://docs.python.org/3.6/library/re.html`.

I will spend the rest of this chapter discussing the application of regular expressions to extract information. In the following sections, you will build a program that, given a set of addresses, extracts the street name of each address.

# Looking for patterns

Creating a good regular expression is a bit of a design process. A regular expression that is too rigid may not be able to match all of the potentially correct matches. On the other hand, a regular expression that is not specific enough may match a large number of strings incorrectly.

The key is to look for a well-defined pattern in the data that easily distinguishes the correct matches from otherwise incorrect matches. It is usually a helpful first step to look through the data itself. This allows you to get an intuitive sense for the existence and frequency of certain patterns.

The following python script uses pandas to read the dataset into a pandas dataframe, extract the address column, and `print` out a random sample of `100` addresses using the pandas `series.sample()` function. A random seed of 0 is used in order to make the resulting printout consistent. The script is available in the external resources as available in the external resources as `explore_addresses.py`.

```
import pandas

## read data to a dataframe
addresses=pandas.read_csv("data/scf_address_data.csv")

## extract address column and print random sample to
## output
print(addresses["address"].sample(100),random_state=0)
```

Note that I could have just used the default printout of the address column rather than a random sample. It's always a good idea, however, to anticipate that the data might be skewed in some way. It's possible that the first `100` addresses have one format while the other addresses have another format. Randomizing the sample ensures that you are able to get a homogeneous view of the data.

After running the previous program, you should see a number of addresses printed out to the Terminal:

```
● ● ●   Terminal
1795          260-300 Osceola Ave S St Paul, MN 55102, USA
707              1054 W Byron St Chicago, IL 60613, USA
5747                6836 Mortenview Dr Taylor, MI 48180, USA
2335          2401-2423 Magnolia St Oakland, CA 94607, USA
4738          6014-6024 Thompson Road East Syracuse, New York
3347              510 6th St Ne Washington, DC 20002, USA
4693          2110 37th Street South Saint Petersburg, Florida
3225                            6518 Stuart Ave Richmond, VA
2868          9060-9270 Railroad Ave Oakland, CA 94603, USA
1887          103 & 105 Misty Morning Way Savannah, Georgia
4453          Spring St. & Market St.  Greensboro, North Car...
2273              230 Quincy Ave Quincy, MA 02169, USA
3933          1823 Berkeley Avenue Saint Paul, Minnesota
4764                3231 Dorr St Toledo, OH 43607, USA
5976                                        800 Howard
6078          110 Dwight St New Haven, CT 06511, USA
                              ...
5555                20th And Telegraph Oakland, California
422           2301-2319 Florin Road Sacramento, California
0                       1718 S. Longmore Mesa, Arizona
1286                            Address Unavailable
345           6211 Buswell Street Richmond, British Columbia
4772          6200-6226 Eastlawn St Oakland, CA 94621, USA
1208          1321-1337 Hambrick Road Stone Mountain, Georgia
5653          8982 Channing Avenue Westminster, California
4335              682 State Route 31 Oswego, Illinois
2031              5940 N Virginia Ave West Ridge
5522              36 Orange St Westfield, Massachusetts
3033                1724 Fulton Rd Nw Canton, Ohio
292               397 2nd St Oakland, CA 94607, USA
5508          1060-1098 North Shore Drive Northeast Saint Pe...
5359          30-42 Elmwood Road Wellesley, Massachusetts
2799                Crown St New Haven, CT, USA
1247          4301-4341 Coliseum Way Oakland, CA 94601, USA
6026              2820 Montana Street Oakland, California
2767              Depalma Court New Haven, Connecticut
339               West Outer Drive Dearborn, Michigan
714               464 3rd Street Albany, New York
2187              361-371 Grand Ave Oakland, CA 94610, USA
2821          100-198 1st Street Southeast Saint Petersburg,...
3359          5720-6266 East Cherokee Drive Canton, Georgia
5820              Riverside Fwy Corona, CA 92882, USA
4599              200 Broadway Fall River, Massachusetts
3348          160 Hilton Avenue Garden City, New York
1532                                3649 N Southport Ave
5551              4022 N Mozart St Irving Park
915               3401 Garland Ave Richmond, Virginia
Name: address, Length: 100, dtype: object
```

Looking over the output, it appears that most addresses fall under the pattern that is standard for US addresses, with the street number first, then the street name, and then the city, state, and zip code.

However, not all of the addresses follow this pattern, for example:

*Spring St. & Market St.  Greensboro, North Car...*
*Pleasant And Main St Malden, Massachusetts*
*Corner Of Lima Ave And Cowan*

It will therefore be important to filter out the entries where the street name cannot be determined by a pattern.

Of the addresses that do fit the standard format, the simplest case seems to be where the street name consists of one word, followed by a street suffix:

*6836 Mortenview Dr Taylor, MI 48180, USA*
*3401 Garland Ave Richmond, Virginia*
*8982 Channing Avenue Westminster, California*
*230 Quincy Ave Quincy, MA 02169, USA*

In this case, the address begins with three components that make up the street address:

*<street number> <initial street name> <street suffix>*

These three components provide an excellent way of pinning down the street name. The street number indicates the beginning of the street name. The street suffix both indicates the end of the street name and confirms that the identified string refers to a street name.

A good approach then would be to identify and extract the street address from the address. From there, the street name, consisting of the initial street name and the street suffix, can be extracted from the street address.

# Quantifying the existence of patterns

If you look through the addresses output from the previous step, you may notice that not all of them have a street address as outlined earlier.

A common deviation from the street address pattern is the addition of an **N** or **S** to a street name. Another deviation is initial street names that contain more than one word:

*3649 N Southport Ave*
*4022 N Mozart St Irving Park*
*260-300 Osceola Ave S St Paul, MN 55102, USA*

*103 & 105 Misty Morning Way Savannah, Georgia*
*1656 Mount Eagle Place Alexandria, Virginia*

Yet another deviation is the omission of street numbers:

*West Outer Drive Dearborn, Michigan*
*Crown St New Haven, CT, USA*

Depending on the project, you will usually need to decide how far to go to capture all of the variations in the data. The more complex the pattern, the more work it will take to capture.

Due to this trade-off, it is helpful to quantify how much of the data is captured by a particular pattern. In the next few subsections, I will walk through the process of creating a pattern string to capture the street address.

# Creating a regular expression to match the street address

Recall that in the street address, you are looking for the following pattern:

> *<street number> <initial street name> <street suffix>*

The first part of the pattern string should match the street number. The street number is a sequence of digits located at the beginning of the string. For the sake of this exercise, I will ignore street addresses that contain letters (such as 10A or 10B) or ranges (such as 110-120). The following should be sufficient to capture the street address:

- A ^ symbol to indicate the beginning of the string
- A [0-9] range to indicate the range of all digits
- A + symbol following the digit range to indicate an indefinitely long sequence of digits
- A \s+ symbol to indicate an arbitrary amount of whitespace afterward

To start off with, in the following demonstration. I will create a Python script called extract_street_names.py. In extract_street_names.py, first the re module and the csv module are imported. Then a pattern string is created to recognize the street street address, starting with the street number:

```
import re
import csv

## match street number at the beginning of string
street_address_pattern_string = "^[0-9]+"
## match space characters
street_address_pattern_string += "\s+"
```

Next, you will add to the pattern string so that it recognizes the initial street same. I will consider the initial street name to be one word. As a large number of street names contain numbers (that is, *1st st, 2nd ave*), the initial street name should be a sequence of characters that are either letters or numbers.

This can be done using the *either or* (|) symbol containing a digit, [0-9], on one side of the | symbol and a letter, [a-z], on the other as the following demonstrates.

```
([a-z]|[0-9])+\s+
```

The + symbol is used to allow the initial street name to be arbitrarily long and the \s+ symbol is used to match an arbitrary amount of white space following the initial street name.

 You do not need to match capital letters here, because I will later use string.lower() function to convert the search string to lower case when matching the pattern.

In the following continuation of extract_street_names.py, the street address pattern string is extended to match the initial street name.

```
import re
import csv

###
### PATTERN STRING FOR MATCHING STREET ADDRESS

## match street number at the beginning of string
street_address_pattern_string = "^[0-9]+"
## match space characters
street_address_pattern_string += "\s+"
## match the street name
street_address_pattern_string += "([0-9]|[a-z])+"
## match space characters
street_address_pattern_string += "\s+"
```

The last step in creating the pattern string is to match the street suffix. Because most street names in the US share a common set of suffixes, the street suffix can be used as a way of verifying that the pattern is a street address and not some other coincidental pattern.

In order to take advantage of this, the approach I will take is to make the pattern more rigid by matching either of a fixed set of street suffixes:

```
"(<suffix1>|<suffix2>|<suffix3>|<suffix4>...)"
```

Since most streets have street suffixes and most suffixes are rather common, this approach should be sufficient to capture a large amount of the data, while verifying that the expression matches a street address. In the following continuation of `extract_street_names.py`, the street address pattern string is further extended to match

```
....
## match the street name
street_address_pattern_string += "[0-9|a-z]+"
## match space characters
street_address_pattern_string += "\s+"

## match common street suffixes:
street_address_pattern_string += "(av|"
street_address_pattern_string += "ave|"
street_address_pattern_string += "avenue|"
street_address_pattern_string += "st|"
street_address_pattern_string += "street|"
street_address_pattern_string += "dr|"
street_address_pattern_string += "rd|"
street_address_pattern_string += "drive|"
street_address_pattern_string += "road|"
street_address_pattern_string += "blvd|"
street_address_pattern_string += "boulevard|"
street_address_pattern_string += "pl|"
street_address_pattern_string += "place)"
```

There's one last step. It isn't likely, but it is possible that some of the street extensions might accidentally pick up on the beginning of a word that starts with the same letters; for example, the words *start*, *stem* and *step* all have `st` at the beginning, and the words *drill*, *drip* and *drone* all start with `dr`. Since it is relatively simple to rule out this possibility, you can verify that the street extension is followed by either a `.` and space, or the end of the string as is done in the following continuation of `extract_street_names.py`:

```
....
street_address_pattern_string += "boulevard|"
street_address_pattern_string += "pl|"
street_address_pattern_string += "place)"
## match whitespace or end of string
street_address_pattern_string += "(\s|$|\.)"
```

Once this is done, the pattern can be compiled as is done in the following continuation of `get_street_names.py`:

```
......
## match whitespace or end of string
street_name_pattern_string += "(\s|$|\.)"

## compile the pattern
street_address_regex = re.compile(street_address_pattern_string)
```

At this stage, the `street_address_regex regular expression` object is capable of matching the street address within a US address string. Now that you've created a regular expression, the next step is to see how it performs when implemented on the data. In the next subsection, you will count the fraction of data entries for which the regular expression produces a match.

# Counting the number of matches

In the following continuation of `extract_street_names.py`, I've opened `scf_address_data.csv` and added a loop to iterate over the rows in the file. Within the loop, each of the addresses are extracted and searched to see if they match the pattern.

Notice that when the regular expression is applied, I use the `.lower()` method to change all capital letters to lowercase. This makes it so that you do not have to account for uppercase letters in the pattern string.

The script keeps a running count of the total number of matches. At the end of the script, the fraction of address strings that match the pattern is printed to the output.

```
....
## compile the pattern
street_address_regex = re.compile(street_address_pattern_string)

## read and iterate over the data
fin = open(with"data/scf_address_data.csv","r")
reader = csv.DictReader(fin)

match_count=0.
for row in reader:
    address=row["address"]
    ## apply the regular expression
    street_address_match = street_address_regex.search(address.lower()):
```

```
    if street_address_match:
        match_count+=1

print("percent match:" + str(match_count/reader.line_num))
fin.close()
```

If everything works correctly, running `extract_street_names.py` should now print out a result of approximately `0.4`. This means that about 40% of the data is captured by the pattern. For the purpose of this exercise, 40% will be plenty of data, though depending on the application, you may require more or less sensitivity.

# Verifying the correctness of the matches

There is no way of objectively quantifying the extent to which the matches are correct without having a better pattern matching tool to begin with. It is a good idea, however, to get a qualitative sense of whether the regular expression is working properly. This can be done by printing out the identified street addresses. Because the `print()` function can slow down the program when working with files, it is good practice to limit the number of `print()` function calls. In the following continuation of `extract_street_names.py`, for addresses that produce a match, the street address is extracted from the address string. Using the `match_count` variable to limit the `print()` function calls, the first 200 street addresses are printed to the output.

```
....
    street_address_match = street_address_regex.search(address.lower()):
    if street_address_match:
        match_count+=1

        street_address = street_address_match.group()
        ## print out the matched items
        ## as a sanity check to make sure
        ## the regular expression is correct
        if match_count<200:
            print(street_address)
....
```

If all goes well, you should see a series of street addresses consisting strictly of a street number, an initial street name, and a street suffix. Here is the output on my machine:

```
○ ● ○  Terminal
52 howe street
20 center street
378 townsend avenue
2720 5th st
2630 5th street
2636 5th street
3032 jenn ave
79 bellerose drive
390 morris ave
41 baylor road
1771 25th st
2490 quebec avenue
404 winchester drive
10 wintergreen avenue
C4100 knoll dr
550 cretin avenue
344 davis st
318 davis st
29 manning street
79 astor pl
637 3rd ave
23 gouverneur st
percent match: 0.4019730660820545
allan@allan-ThinkPad-W510 ~/Documents/book/ch5/ch5 $
```

From the result the regular expression appears to be effective at identifying street addresses in address strings. The last step is identify and extract the street name from the string containing the street address. This is done in the next section.

# Extracting patterns

There are a few approaches that can be used to extract the street name from the street address. The one I will use here is to make a regular expression to recognize just the street number. The street number regular expression can be used to split the street address string. In the resulting array, the second entry should contain the street name.

In the following continuation of `extract_street_addresses.py`, an additional regular expression is created to match just the street number and the following white space. Within the for loop that iterates over the data, the `street_number_regex` regular expression is used to split the `street_address` string into two components, the second of which contains the street name:

```
....
### JUST THE STREET NUMBER
## match street number at the beginning of string
```

```
street_number_pattern_string = "^[0-9]+"
## match space characters
street_number_pattern_string += "\s+"

## compile the pattern
street_address_regex = re.compile(street_address_pattern_string)
street_number_regex = re.compile(street_number_pattern_string)
....
....
        street_address=street_address_match.group()
        street_name = street_number_regex.split(street_address)[1]

        ## as a sanity check to make sure
        ## the regular expression is correct
        ## print out the matched items.
        if row_count<200:
            # print(street_address)
            print(street_name)
....
```

Running `extract_street_addresses.py` at this should produce a printout of reliable street names. In the next step, I will output a new file with an additional column containing the newly extracted street names.

# Outputting the data to a new file

The last step is to save the results of applying the regular expression. In the following continuation of `extract_street_names.py`, an output CSV file called `scf_street_name_data.csv` is opened with write permission. This time, I've use a `DictWriter` object, which writes dictionaries to the output instead of Python lists:

```
....
## read and iterate over the data
fin=open("data/scf_address_data.csv","r",newline="")
fout=open("data/scf_street_name_data.csv","w",newline="")
reader = csv.DictReader(fin)

headers=reader.fieldnames
headers.append("street_name")
writer = csv.DictWriter(fout,fieldnames=headers)

....
....
fin.close()
fout.close()
```

Now the program is finally set up to write new data to the output file.

In this demonstration, only the data entries that produce a street name are written to the output file. In the following continuation of `extract_street_names.py`, for each row where a street name is produced, the street name is added to the data entry. The resulting data entry is written as a row to the output CSV file:

. . . .

```
        street_address=street_address_match.group()
        street_name = street_number_regex.split(street_address)[1]
        ## append the street address to the
        ## row and write result to the output
        row["street_name"] = street_name
        writer.writerow(row)
```

. . . .

That's it! You've extracted the street name from addresses. If all goes well, running `extract_street_names.py` should output a new file with a new column for street names:

# Summary

In this chapter, you've learned how to implement regular expressions in Python. In addition, you've learned a process for identifying patterns and building appropriate pattern strings to recognizing particular patterns. To summarize, the first step to approaching a pattern recognition problem is to observe the data and Identify a pattern that can be represented with a regular expression. Once a pattern has been identified, the next step is to build a pattern string to capture the data and verify that the pattern string works well and as expected. Finally, the regular expression should be implemented expression to either clean, extract or filter text data.

This concludes the initial section of the book dealing with a generalized programming approach to data wrangling. In the next two chapters, I will take on a more formulated approach to data wrangling.

In the next chapter, `Chapter 6`, Cleaning *Numerical Data - An Introduction to R and RStudio*, I will introduce the R programming language and IDE, and then show how to use R to conduct common numerical data cleaning tasks.

# 6

# Cleaning Numerical Data - An Introduction to R and RStudio

The philosophy behind the previous chapters leading up to this point has been to take a generalized programming approach to data wrangling. A good grasp of the underlying programming techniques involved in manipulating data gives you the ability to tackle non-standard problems in data wrangling when they are encountered.

However, a large number of tasks can be more concisely and elegantly expressed with a language specific to data manipulation. In many cases, the R environment and programming language can allow you to express more with less. On top of that, several packages built on top of R can make the language even more concise and expressive. In this chapter and the next, I will show you how R can be used to take a more formulated approach to data wrangling. This chapter will be an introduction to R with the application of numerical data cleaning. This chapter will include the following sections:

- Logistical overview
- Introducing R and RStudio
- Familiarizing yourself with R and RStudio
- Conducting basic outlier detection and removal
- Handling NA values
    - Deleting missing values
    - Replacing missing values with a constant
    - Imputation of missing values

Lastly, at the end of the chapter will be a section to list the variable names used in the chapter and their contents.

# Logistical overview

All of the activities in this chapter will be conducted in a single R script. R scripts are files with the .R extension which are analogous to Python scripts. This chapter will make use of the RStudio IDE rather than a text editor for editing code, so you will be able to create this script from within RStudio (I will explain how to do this later in the chapter).

The R script containing the code for this chapter is called r_intro.R and is available in the code folder of the external resources. All external resources are available at the following link: https://goo.gl/8S58ra.

# Data

The dataset for *Chapter 6* will be the artificial_roads_by_region.csv dataset that was introduced in *Chapter 4*. It can be downloaded from the **data** folder of the external resources.

# Directory structure

To follow along with the exercises in Chapter 6, *Cleaning Numerical Data - An Introduction to R and RStudio*, create a project folder called ch6. The ch6 folder should have a folder called data, which should contain the artificial_roads_by_region.csv dataset used with this chapter. The project folder will contain an R script called r_intro.R; however, there is no need to create the file beforehand, since you can create and save R scripts from RStudio. The following is the directory structure for this chapter:

```
ch6/
--> r_intro.R
--> data/
----> artificial_roads_by_region.csv
```

# Installing R and RStudio

For this chapter and the next, you will need to install both the RStudio IDE and R base. R base is the core R programming language and environment and is needed in order to use RStudio. Installation instructions for both RStudio and R base are available in the *Installation* document of the external resources.

# Introducing R and RStudio

**R** is a programming language and environment for statistical computing and graphics. R differs from Python in that it is specialized for statistical computing and contains a number of features in addition to the programming language. The R project website lists the features of R as:

- An effective data handling and storage facility
- A suite of operators for calculations on arrays - in particular, matrices
- A large, coherent, integrated collection of intermediate tools for data analysis
- Graphical facilities for data analysis and display either onscreen or on hard copy
- A well-developed, simple and effective programming language that includes conditionals, loops, user-defined recursive functions, and input and output facilities

The most common way of using R is through **RStudio**, an IDE for interfacing with the R programming language and environment. RStudio combines several components to centralize and facilitate the process of working with data. These include:

- A console for executing R commands:

```
Console  ~/Documents/book/ch6/ch6/  ⇨
> 1+1
[1] 2
>
```

- An editor for writing and executing code and viewing data:

```
r_intro.R ×
                Source on Save     Q      ▼          ▼          Run          Source  ▼
 1  ####
 2  ####
 3  ## vector intro
 4  print(c(1,2,3,4,5,6))
 5  print(1:6)
 6
 7  my.vector=1:10
 8  print(my.vector)
 9  print(my.vector[3])
10  print(my.vector[1:5])
11
12  ## is.na example
13  print(is.na(c(1,NA,2,NA,NA,3,4,NA,5)))
14
15  ####
16  ####
17  ## reading in data
18  ## set the working directory
19  ## the working directory here should be changed
20  ## for your setup
21  setwd('~/Documents/book/ch6/ch6/')
22
23  ## Read in the data, and assign to the roads_by_country
24  ## variable. Roads by country is an R Dataframe
```

- A panel to show the variables, dataframes, and functions in the current environment:

```
Environment    History

        Import Dataset ▾                                     List ▾
   Global Environment ▾                             Q
Data
  roads              1000 obs. of 13 variables
    region.name: Factor w/ 1000 levels "AADIOXNVYB","AAULMSPHDA",..:
    X2011 : num NA 1137 NA 1415 4054 ...
    X2010 : num NA 1117 1049 NA 4038 ...
    X2009 : num NA NA NA NA NA ...
    X2008 : num NA 1078 NA 1361 NA ...
    X2007 : num NA NA NA NA NA ...
    X2006 : num 1222 NA NA NA 3971 ...
    X2005 : num NA NA NA NA NA ...
    X2004 : num NA 998 NA 1288 NA ...
    X2003 : num 1183 NA NA 1269 NA ...
    X2002 : num NA 959 NA NA 3905 ...
    X2001 : num NA NA 918 1233 NA ...
```

- A panel to display, among other things, graphs and help information:

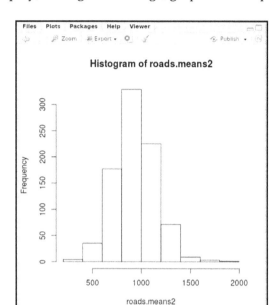

In the next section, I will walk through some of the features of R and RStudio.

# Familiarizing yourself with RStudio

Compared to RStudio, the Python development process that has been used in previous chapters has been a bit indirect. Code has been written in a text editor to perform a particular function and then executed as a whole through a separate interface.

Writing code in RStudio is more of an iterative process. Code can be run line by line from the editor, and data and variables are stored continuously within the environment. This means that you can conduct analysis, observe the data, and verify the correctness of your code as you go. The following steps can be used to create an R script in RStudio.

1. To begin with, open the RStudio program:

2. From RStudio, you can create a new R script by selecting **File** | **New** | **Rscript**. This will create and open a .R file in the text editor:

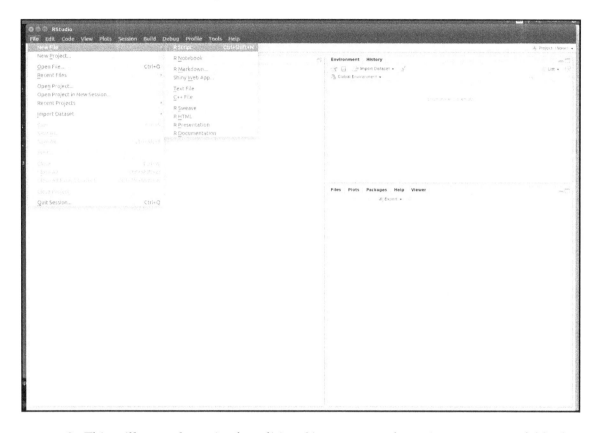

3. This will open the script for editing. You can save the script to your ch6 folder by selecting **File** | **Save**. The name of the script is not that important here, but I will name mine r_intro. Note that RStudio will add the file extension automatically:

# Running R commands

Commands in R can be entered directly into the console, but they can also be run line by line from the editor. To run a line of code from the editor, you can move the cursor to that line, and press *Ctrl + Enter* on your keyboard.

Try entering `1+1` in your R script and pressing *Ctrl + Enter*, with the cursor on that line. The following should be printed in the console:

```
Console    ~/Documents/book/ch6/ch6/
> 1+1
[1] 2
>
```

# Setting the working directory

Like the terminal, the R environment interacts with the filesystem relative to a particular directory. In R, the directory can be set directly in the script using the `setwd()` function.

It is helpful to set the working directory at the beginning of an R script to the location of the data. For this chapter, the working directory should be set to the `ch6` project folder. I've added the following line to the beginning of my script - note that the path you use should be specific to the way your file system is set up:

```
setwd("~/Documents/book/ch6/ch6/")
```

In R, the forward slash / character can be used regardless of operating system. After adding a line to set the working directory, you can execute the line by moving the cursor to that line and pressing *Ctrl + Enter*. Alternatively, you can highlight some or all of the text from one or more lines and press *Ctrl + Enter* to execute the code. If the command works, you should see the line printed in the console below the editor. You can verify that the working directory is set correctly by entering `getwd()` into the console as follows:

```
Console    ~/Documents/book/ch6/ch6/
> setwd("~/Documents/book/ch6/ch6/")
> getwd()
[1] "/home/allan/Documents/book/ch6/ch6"
>
```

# Reading data

You can read a CSV dataset into the R environment using the `read.csv()` function, which accepts a path string to a CSV file and returns an R dataframe. Variable assignment in R is done using the `<-` symbol, which is more or less analogous to the = symbol in Python. After the working directory is properly set, the following line will read `artificial_roads_by_region.csv` and assign the resulting data to an R dataframe called `roads`:

```
roads <- read.csv("data/artificial_roads_by_region.csv")
```

# The R dataframe

The R dataframe is a built-in data structure that represents tabular data. Once a dataframe is created, the columns and initial values of the dataframe can be viewed in the **Environment** tab in the upper left corner of RStudio:

Double-clicking on a dataframe listed in the **Environment** tab will display a spreadsheet of the data in the editor panel:

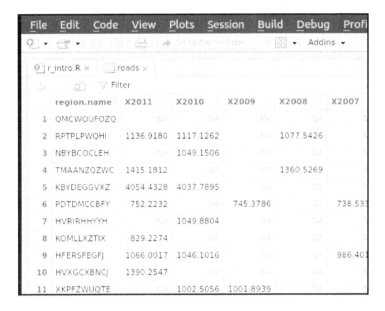

At this point, I will point out that the column names have been changed from the original CSV. `Region name` has become `region.name` and `2011` has become `X2011`. R uses the column header names as variables, so the column names need to be changed to proper variables names. It is possible to change the column names that R uses with the `colnames()` function, though I will keep the names that R assigned.

In R, the `.` character is valid as a part of a variable name, so long as it is followed by a letter. Variables in R often contain `.` characters to separate words.

# R vectors

Vectors in R are analogous to Python lists - they are a data structure that contains an ordered list of values. A vector can be created using the following syntax:

```
vector <- c(<element1>, <element2>, <element3>)
```

Try entering the following in your R console:

```
> c(1,2,3,4,5,6)
```

It is also possible to create a vector consisting of a sequence of numbers using the following syntax:

```
sequence_of_numbers <- <start_number>:<finish_number>
```

Try entering the following into your R console:

```
> 1:5
```

Vectors can be indexed using integer numbers or other vectors. For example, the following creates a vector called `my.vector`, prints the third value of `my.vector`, and then prints the first five values of `my.vector`:

```
my.vector=1:10
print(my.vector)
print(my.vector[3])
print(my.vector[1:5])
```

 Indexing in R starts with 1, so be sure not to get this mixed up with Python indexing, which starts at 0.

# Indexing R dataframes

Individual columns can be selected from a dataframe using the $ symbol. The following selects the data from `2011` from the `roads` dataframe:

```
roads.2011 = roads$X2011
```

The resulting value is an R vector containing the values of the selected column.

Dataframes can also be indexed by `row` and `column` using the following syntax:

```
new.dataframe <- original.dataframe[<row_index>,<column index>].
```

To select all `rows` or all `columns`, the `row_index` or `column_index` can be left blank. For example:

```
the.same.thing <- roads[,]
```

The rows and columns indices can both be an integer value or a vector of integer values. For example:

```
first.three.rows <- roads[1:3,]
first.three.columns <- roads[,1:3]
```

Row and column indices can also be a vector of logical values, as I will demonstrate later. Finally, the column index can be a vector of column names. For example:

```
X2011.with.region <- roads[,c("region.name","X2011")]
```

In the next section, I'll show you how to use the tools that I've demonstrated so far to perform the task from `Chapter` 4, *Reading, Analyzing, Modifying, and Writing Data - Part II*, of finding the `2011` total road length.

# Finding the 2011 total in R

Let's revisit the task of finding the `2011` total, this time using R. The first step is to extract the `X2011` values. This has already been done in a previous step, which created the `roads.2011` vector.

The next step is to find the sum of all of the values in the `roads.2011` vector. One easy way is to use the built in R `sum()` function with a parameter that skips over NA values. I will show how to use the `sum()` function in this way this section (feel free to skip ahead if you want the short cut).

First however, I will take a more round about approach to demonstrate the use of indexing. This will involve removing the NA values manually from the `roads.2011` vector and then applying the `sum()` function.

You can create a vector of logical values using the `is.na()` function. The `is.na()` function takes as an argument a vector or dataframe and returns a vector or dataframe, respectively, of TRUE or FALSE values indicating whether the value of a position is NA. For example, you can try entering the following into the console:

```
> is.na(c(1,NA,2,NA,NA,3,4,NA,5))
```

You can create a vector of logical values corresponding to the NA values of `roads.2011` using the `is.na()` function. The resulting vector can then be used to index and extract the non-NA values of the `roads.2011` vector.

In the following line, a vector called `not.na` is created. The resulting `not.na` vector is a vector of logical values in which `TRUE` corresponds to an index of `roads.2011` which is not `NA` and `FALSE` corresponds to an index of `roads.2011` which is `NA`. The `!` symbol is used to flip the `TRUE` and `FALSE` values so that `TRUE` corresponds to non-`NA` values.

```
not.na <- !is.na(total.2011)
```

Using an array of logical values to index a vector or a dataframe will extract all of the indices corresponding to a `TRUE` value. The following line will create a vector of all of the non-NA values in the `roads.2011` vector:

```
roads.2011.cleaned <- roads.2011[not.na]TRUE and FALSE values so that TRUE
corresponds to non-NA values._
```

Finally, the `sum()` function can be used to add the values:

```
total.2011<-sum(roads.2011.cleaned)
```

The more concise way of finding the sum is to set the `na.rm` of the sum function to `TRUE`, so that the function will skip over the `NA` values:

```
total.2011<-sum(roads.2011, na.rm=TRUE)
```

From the beginning, the following is the sequence of steps that have been used to read the data and find the 2011 total:

```
####
####
## reading in data
## set the working directory
## the working directory here should be changed
## for your setup
setwd("path/to/your/project/folder")

## Read in the data, and assign to the roads_by_country
## variable. Roads by country is an R Dataframe
roads <- read.csv("data/artificial_roads_by_region.csv")

## select the 2011 column from the roads dataframe
roads.2011 <- roads$X2011

####
####
## finding the 2011 total

## create a index corresponding to not na values
not.na <- !is.na(roads.2011)
```

```
## index roads.2011 using not na
roads.2011.cleaned <- roads.2011[not.na]

## print the sum of the available roads in 2011.
total.2011<-sum(roads.2011.cleaned)

## the more concise way
total.2011<-sum(roads.2011, na.rm=TRUE)
```

Finding the sum of a column is a useful exercise in data manipulation; however, it may not be enough to get an accurate estimate, particularly if there is a high number of missing or erroneous values. (I created this particular dataset, so I can assure you that there are a number of missing and erroneous values.) In the following sections, I will go over some common techniques to clean numerical data. This will help to get more accurate results for the 2011 total, but it will also demonstrate some additional features of R and RStudio.

Before I get into the numerical data cleaning process, I will warn you that the variable names can get confusing, because there are several layers of filtering that take place. It is hard to represent all of these layers with a descriptive variable naming convention. The `dplyr` package, which I will introduce in the next chapter, will help considerably to keep R code concise and descriptive. For now, you can refer to a list of all of the variable names and their content at the end of the chapter.

# Conducting basic outlier detection and removal

**Outlier detection** is a field of study in its own right, and deals with the detection of data that does not fit in a particular dataset. Advanced outlier detection techniques can be considered a part of data wrangling, but often draw from other fields, such as statistics and machine learning. For the purposes of this book, I will conduct a very basic form of outlier detection to find values that are too high. Values that are too high might be aggregates of the data or might reflect erroneous entries.

In these next few steps, you will use the built-in plotting functionality in R to observe the data and look for particularly high values.

The first step is to put the data in a form that can be easily visualized. A simple technique to capture the trend in the data by row is to find the means of all of the non-NA values in each data entry. This can be done using the `rowMeans()` function in R.

Before using the `roawMeans()` function, you will need to remove all of the non-numerical features - in this case, the `region.name` column. It is possible to index all of the columns except for one, by including a – sign before the index. The following creates a new dataframe without the `region.name` column:

```
roads.num <- roads[,-1]
```

The `num` in the `roads.num` dataframe stands for *numerical* because the `roads.num` dataframe just contains the *numerical* data.

With the first column removed, you can use the `rowMeans` function to obtain a vector with the mean value of each row. Like the `sum()` function, the `rowMeans()` function accepts an `na.rm` parameter which will cause the function to ignore NA values. The following returns a vector with the mean value across each row:

```
roads.means <- rowMeans( roads.num , na.rm=TRUE )
```

To get a sense for how the data is distributed, you can plot a histogram of the means by using the `hist()` function as follows:

```
hist(roads.means)
```

In the lower right-hand corner of RStudio, you should see a histogram that is quite skewed towards the left. The following is the output on my computer:

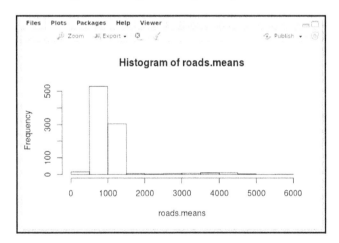

There appears to be a small number of values that are far to the right of the central distribution. Deciding what should be removed should usually be justified based on the particular project and the context of the data.

However, since this particular dataset doesn't quite have a context (it was randomly generated), I will remove the data that doesn't follow the general trend. The main distribution seems to go from zero to about 0 to 2000, so I will remove all of the rows with a mean greater than 2000.

To remove the rows whose means are greater than 2000, you can first create an index vector of logical values corresponding to row means less than 2000 as follows:

```
roads.keep <- roads.means < 2000
```

Finally, you can use the logical vector from the previous step to index the original `roads` dataframe. The following removes all of the rows with means greater than 2000:

```
## remove entries with means greater than 2000
roads.keep <- roads.means < 2000

## remove outliers from the original dataframe
roads2<-roads[roads.keep,]

## remove outliers from the numerical roads dataframe
roads.num2 <- roads.num[roads.keep,]

## remove outliers from the vector of means
## (we will use this later)
roads.means2 <- roads.means[roads.keep]

## plot the means with outliers removed
hist(roads.means2)
```

Plotting a histogram of the filtered row means now yields a recognizable normal distribution:

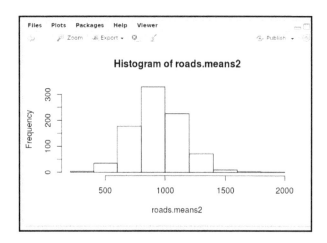

Now that the erroneous values are removed, the next step is to handle the missing values.

# Handling NA values

Sometimes, it is acceptable to have NA values in the dataset. However, for many types of analysis, NA values need to be either removed or replaced. In the case of road length, a better estimate of total road length could be generated if the NA values were replaced with best guesses. In the following subsections, I will walk through these three approaches to handling NA values:

- Deletion
- Insertion
- Imputation

# Deleting missing values

The simplest way to handle NA values is to delete any entry that contains an NA value, or a certain number of NA values. When removing entries with NA values, there is a trade-off between the correctness of the data and the completeness of the data. Data entries that contain NA values may also contain several useful non-NA values, and and removing too many data entries could reduce the dataset to a point where it is no longer useful.

For this dataset, it is not that important to have all of the years present; even one year is enough to give us a rough idea of how much road length is in the particular region at any point over the 12 years. A safe approach for this particular application would be to remove all of the rows where all of the values are NA.

A quick shortcut to finding the rows for which all values are NA is to use the rowSums() function. The rowSums() function finds the sum of each row, and takes a parameter to ignore NA values. The following finds the sum of the non-NA values in the roads.num2 dataframe:

```
roads.num2.rowsums <- rowSums(roads.num2,na.rm=TRUE)
```

Because NA values are ignored, in the resulting vector of row sums, a 0 corresponds to either a row with all NA values or a region with no roads. In either case, a 0 value corresponds to a row that is not important and can be filtered out. The following creates an index that can be used to filter out all such rows:

```
roads.keep3 <- roads.num2.rowsums > 0
```

In the following continuation of `r_intro.R`, the `roads.keep3` vector is used to filter out the rows that have either all `NA` values or 0 roads:

```
roads3 <- roads2[roads.keep2,]
roads.num3 <- roads.num2[roads.keep2,]
roads.means3 <- roads.means3
```

Next, I will do a quick demonstration of another approach to `NA` handling, replacing the values with a constant.

# Replacing missing values with a constant

Replacing all `NA` values with a constant is actually rather simple. A dataframe can be indexed using another dataframe of logical values of the same dimension. The following will create a new dataframe that is a copy of `roads3` and replace all of the `NA` values with 0:

```
roads.replace.na <- roads3
roads.replace.na[is.na(roads3)] <- 0
```

In this chapter, I won't use the dataframe with replaced `NA` values which was just created, so this is just for demonstration purposes. A more effective way to handle `NA` values, when possible, is to replace the missing value with an estimate based on existing data.

# Imputation of missing values

A good guess for the missing values is the mean value of the non-NA values in the same row (in a particular region), since the total length of road doesn't change all that much year to year.

In the following continuation of `r_intro.R`, the row means in indices corresponding to `NA` values in 2011 are extracted from the `roads.means3` vector. The extracted row means are then assigned to the indices of the `roads.2011.3` vector which correspond to `NA` values:

```
roads.2011.3 <- roads3$X2011
roads.2011.3[is.na(roads.2011.3)] <- roads.means3[is.na(roads.2011.3)]
print(sum(roads.2011.3))
```

This results in a much better estimate of the total roads length as of 2011. It is possible to go even further however to get a similar estimate for each column.

There are a number of ways to approach the task of getting an estimate for each column. The approach I will take is to go column by column and replace each of the NA values in that column with the corresponding mean value for the corresponding row.

This can be done with the `apply()` function, which applies a function to each column. Before using the `apply()` function, you will need to create the function that is applied to each column. Functions in R work similarly to functions in Python, but have a different syntax. The following is the syntax for a function in R:

```
my.function <- function(<arguments>){
    <code block>
    return(result)
}
```

The following is a function called `impute()` which takes two arguments: a vector that is a column of a dataframe, and a vector of equal length that contains the imputation values for each row. The `impute` function returns the original dataframe column where the NA values have been replaced with the corresponding imputation values:

```
impute <- function(x,imputations) {
    x[is.na(x)] <- imputations[is.na(x)]
    return(x)
}
```

The `apply()` function takes as its first argument a dataframe, and its third argument a function. The second argument to the `apply()` function is a 1 if the function should be applied to each row, or a 2 if the function should be applied to each column. After the third argument, all additional arguments to the `apply()` function are passed into the function which is specified in the third argument. The `apply()` function returns a data type called a **matrix**, so the result will need to be converted back to a dataframe using the `data.frame()` function.

In the following continuation of `r_intro.R` the `apply()` function is used to go column by column, run the impute function on each column, and return a result with the imputed values:

```
## apply the impute function to each column with apply()
roads.impute.na <- data.frame(
  apply(roads3,2,impute,imputations=roads.means3)
)
print(colSums(roads.impute.na))
```

The resulting dataframe--`roads.impute.na`--is now a dataframe containing imputed values in the place of the `NA` values. Printing the column sums with the `colSums()` function should reveal the estimated total road length for each year in the console output:

```
+    return(as.numeric(x))
+ }
> roads.impute.na <- data.frame(
+    apply(roads.num3,2,impute,imputations=roads.means3)
+ )
> colSums(roads.impute.na)
   X2011    X2010    X2009    X2008    X2007    X2006    X2005    X2004    X2003    X2002    X2001    X2000
808648.3 807977.9 805344.1 802956.2 801247.2 799160.9 797380.7 795128.1 793213.5 790691.5 788098.0 786618.5
>
```

# Variable names and contents

- `roads`: The R dataframe containing the original data
- `roads.2011`: The 2011 column of the roads dataframe
- `not.na`: An array of logical that corresponds to the non-NA values of the 2011 column
- `roads.2011.cleaned`: The 2011 column from the roads dataframe with the `NA` values removed
- `total.2011`: The sum of the 2011 values
- `roads.num`: The roads dataframe without the first column (just the numerical data)
- `roads.means`: A vector containing the mean value of each row
- `roads.keep`: A vector of logical that is True for rows for which the mean is less than 2000 (non-outliers)
- `roads2`: The roads dataframe with outliers removed
- `roads.num2`: The roads dataframe with the first column removed (just the numerical data) and the outliers removed
- `roads.means2`: The vector of means with outliers removed
- `roads.num2.rowsums`: The sum of the values in each row with the outliers removed (where a sum of 0 indicates that all values in the row are NA)
- `roads.keep2`: A logical vector used to index the rows for which there is at least one non-NA value
- `roads3`: The roads dataframe with outliers removed and the rows with all `NA` values removed

- `roads.num3`: The roads dataframe with the first column removed (just the numerical data) and the outliers removed, and with rows containing all NA values removed
- `roads.means3`: The vector of means with outliers removed, and with rows containing all NA values removed
- `roads.replace.na`: The roads dataframe with outliers removed, the rows with all NA values removed, and the NA values replaced with 0
- `impute`: A function that takes a vector with NA values and a vector with replacement values of the same length, and returns the original vector with the NAs replaced
- `roads.impute.na`: The roads dataframe with outliers removed, the rows with all NA values removed, and the NA values replaced with the row mean

# Summary

In summary, this has been a brief introduction to R, but it just scratches the surface of the features of the R language. R is a fully functional programming language, so there are quite a few ways to approach any given problem. In the Links and Further Reading document of the external resources, I've provided some links that go into more depth on the R language. The external resources are available at `https://goo.gl/8S58ra`.

In the next chapter, I will introduce the `dplyr` package for R. The `dplyr` documentation refers to `dplyr` as a "grammar for data manipulation". The `dplyr` package can be used to express a number of data manipulation operations in a neat and concise manner.

# 7
# Simplifying Data Manipulation with dplyr

Both R and pandas go a step further to make data manipulation a bit more expressive than most programming languages. For example, many iterative tasks that would otherwise require a for loop (such as selecting a column) can be done using a single line of code.

However, there are still aspects of data manipulation that could be expressed a bit more directly. Recall that in previous chapter, a number of processing steps and variables were used to filter the data and find the result. It can be hard to express a large number of data manipulation operations in a way that is descriptive and contained.

Ideally, it should be possible to express each of the steps for processing data in one sequence of code, and in a way that reflects the function of each processing step. A number of packages build on the R programming language and environment in order to make it more expressive, concise, neat, and consistent. One well developed effort to make data processing in R more elegant and intuitive is a collection of packages collectively called the **tidyverse**.

At the time of writing this, the tidyverse includes five packages, two of which I will be using in this chapter:

- `tibble` is just another version of R's dataframe that has a few improvements. In particular, the printout is a bit cleaner.
- `dplyr`, as the documentation states, is a grammar for data manipulation. It contains a series of functions that allow you to express data manipulation operations easily and intuitively. The syntax for using `dplyr` takes some getting used to.

The tidyverse also includes a few more packages that may be of use, but I won't cover all of them here. Excellent documentation on all of the tidyverse packages is available at `https://www.tidyverse.org`.

In this chapter, I will walk through some of the basic functionality of the `dplyr` package and show how it can be used to manipulate data. This chapter will include the following sections:

- Logistical overview
- Introducing `dplyr`
- Getting started with `dplyr`
- Chaining operations together
- Filtering the rows of a dataframe
- Summarizing data by category
- Rewriting code using `dplyr`

# Logistical overview

As in the previous chapter, all exercises will be completed using a single R script called `dplyr_intro.R`. This chapter will include two demonstrations. The first of these is a comparison of fuel economy and gas prices. The second demonstration is a rewrite of some of the work from *Chapter 6* using the `dplyr` library.

The finished product from this chapter, along with all of the exercises from this book, is available in the code folder of the external resources. All of the external resources in this book can be accessed from the Google Drive folder at the following link: `https://goo.gl/8S58ra`.

# Data

For the demonstrations in this chapter three datasets will be used. The first of these is a dataset of fuel economy data for various vehicle models. The fuel economy dataset is made available by the U.S. Department of Energy. The fuel economy dataset has a large number of non descriptive data variables, so I've also included a link to the description of the data in the external resources.

The second dataset used is a dataset of gas prices, made available by the U.S. Department of Labor, Bureau of Labor Statistics.

The third dataset is the artificial road length data used in the previous chapters. This dataset contains the total amount of road length by year in hypothetical regions of a hypothetical country.

All three datasets can be accessed and downloaded from the *data* folder in the external resources.

# File system setup

As with the previous chapter, this chapter only requires a single project folder called `ch7` with a data folder called `data`. All datasets for this chapter should be placed in the `data` folder. The R script for this chapter should be created from within R and saved in the `ch7` project folder.

# Installing the dplyr and tibble packages

You can install an R package by entering the `install.packages()` function into the RStudio console, with the package name as a parameter. To install `dplyr` and `tibble`, enter the following commands into the console:

```
> install.packages('dplyr')
> install.packages('tibble')
```

That's it!

Just in case anything changes, I've included installation instructions in the external resources as well.

# Introducing dplyr

According to the `dplyr` documentation at `http://dplyr.tidyverse.org/`, `dplyr` is a grammar of data manipulation, providing a consistent set of verbs that help you solve the most common data manipulation challenges, as follows:

- `mutate()`: Adds new variables that are functions of existing variables
- `select()`: Picks variables based on their names
- `filter()`: Picks cases based on their values
- `summarize()`: Reduces multiple values down to a single summary

- `arrange()`: Changes the ordering of the rows
- `group_by()`: Allows you to perform any operation by group

While each of the *verbs* corresponds to a particular function in `dplyr`, a verb can be thought of more generally as particular action that transform the data in a certain way.

 In addition to the verbs listed here, there is also functionality in dplyr that can be used to *merge* (or *join*) data from different sources though I won't be covering these features here.

In the following sections, I will demonstrate each of these functions individually through two demonstrations. In the first of these demonstrations, I will use `dplyr` to process data about fuel economy and gas prices. Ultimately, I will use the process data to create visualizations that compare trends in fuel economy to trends in gas prices.

# Getting started with dplyr

To start off with, I will create an R script called `dplyr_intro.R` and set up my R environment. First, you should set your working directory to the `ch7` project folder. Next, you should read the fuel economyhttps://catalog.data.gov/dataset/consumer-price-index-average-price-data dataset into a dataframe as follows:

```
setwd("path/to/your/project/folder")
vehicles<-read.csv("data/vehicles.csv")
```

The next step is to import the `dplyr` and `tibble` packages. In R, you can import a package using the `library()` function. The following lines import the `dplyr` package and the `tibble` package:

```
library('dplyr')
library('tibble')
```

I will start with the `select()` function. The `select()` function allows you to *select* a certain number of columns from a dataframe and returns another dataframe containing only those selected columns. As its first argument, the `select()` function takes a dataframe. The following arguments to the `select()` function after the first argument are the names of the columns to be selected from the original dataframe. The result is a dataframe containing only the selected columns.

Though I won't be using them here, dplyr provides a few functions to make it possible to select columns as a function of their name or position. These include starts_with(), ends_with(), contains(), matches() and num_range(). These functions can be helpful when working with datasets that contain a large number of columns. Details are available in the documentation at http://dplyr.tidyverse.org/reference/select. html.

With the fuel economy dataset, one use of the select() function might be to create a dataframe that just contains the product details for each car. In the following continuation of dplyr_intro.R, I use the select() function to select the make, model, and year columns from the vehicles dataframe:

```
vehicles.product <- select(data,make,model,year)
print(Vehicles.product)
```

Running the previous lines should create a dataframe containing just the product information and produce a printout of the dataframe as follows:

```
Console  ~/Documents/book/ch7/ch7/
302                     Dodge                          D250 Pickup 2WD 1993
303                     GMC          Safari 2WD (passenger) 1985
304                     Dodge                          D250 Pickup 2WD 1993
305                     Jeep              Comanche Pickup 4WD 1993
306                     Jeep              Comanche Pickup 4WD 1993
307                     Jeep              Comanche Pickup 4WD 1993
308                     Jeep              Comanche Pickup 4WD 1993
309                     Ford                     F150 Pickup 2WD 1993
310                     Ford                     F150 Pickup 2WD 1993
311                     Ford                     F150 Pickup 2WD 1993
312                     Ford                     F150 Pickup 2WD 1993
313                     Ford                     F150 Pickup 2WD 1993
314                     Toyota                          Van 2WD 1985
315                     Ford                     F150 Pickup 2WD 1993
316                     Ford                     F150 Pickup 2WD 1993
317                     Ford                     F150 Pickup 2WD 1993
318                     Ford                     F250 Pickup 2WD 1993
319                     Ford                     F250 Pickup 2WD 1993
320                     Ford                     F250 Pickup 2WD 1993
321                     Ford                     F250 Pickup 2WD 1993
322                     Ford                     F250 Pickup 2WD 1993
323                     Ford                     F250 Pickup 2WD 1993
324                     Ford                     F250 Pickup 2WD 1993
325                     Toyota                          Van 2WD 1985
326                     Ford                 Ranger Pickup 2WD 1993
327                     Ford                 Ranger Pickup 2WD 1993
328                     Ford                 Ranger Pickup 2WD 1993
329                     Ford                 Ranger Pickup 2WD 1993
330                     Ford                 Ranger Pickup 2WD 1993
331                     Ford                 Ranger Pickup 2WD 1993
332                     GMC                      Sierra 1500 2WD 1993
333                     GMC                      Sierra 1500 2WD 1993
 [ reached getOption("max.print") -- omitted 38937 rows ]
>
```

You can make the printout a bit more elegant by converting the result to a `tibble` object as follows:

```
## the same thing as a tibble
vehicles.product.as.tibble <- as_tibble(
  select(vehicles,make,model,year)
)
print(vehicles.product.as.tibble)
```

Printing out the `tibble` version of the dataframe, as is done in the previous lines, will produce a much cleaner result, as follows:

```
> print(vehicles.product.as.tibble)
# A tibble: 39,270 x 3
              make                  model  year
            <fctr>                 <fctr> <int>
1  Alfa Romeo   Spider Veloce 2000   1985
2     Ferrari           Testarossa   1985
3       Dodge              Charger   1985
4       Dodge B150/B250 Wagon 2WD   1985
5      Subaru    Legacy AWD Turbo   1993
6      Subaru               Loyale   1993
7      Subaru               Loyale   1993
8      Toyota              Corolla   1993
9      Toyota              Corolla   1993
10     Toyota              Corolla   1993
# ... with 39,260 more rows
>
```

Now that the product information for each of the data entries is available, it may be helpful to arrange the rows in a particular order. Arranging the order of the rows could be particularly helpful if the data will need to be viewed or processed manually.

The `arrange()` function arranges the rows in a particular order by column. The following code will arrange the vehicle product data first by make, then by model, and then by year:

```
vehicles.product.arranged <- as.tibble(
  arrange(vehicles.product,make,model,year)
)
print(vehicles.product.arranged)
```

The *arranged* version of the product data is organized in alphabetical order by make and model, and then by year, as follows:

```
> print(vehicles.product.arranged)
# A tibble: 39,270 x 3
      make        model  year
     <fctr>       <fctr> <int>
 1  Acura 2.2CL/3.0CL  1997
 2  Acura 2.2CL/3.0CL  1997
 3  Acura 2.2CL/3.0CL  1997
 4  Acura 2.3CL/3.0CL  1998
 5  Acura 2.3CL/3.0CL  1998
 6  Acura 2.3CL/3.0CL  1998
 7  Acura 2.3CL/3.0CL  1999
 8  Acura 2.3CL/3.0CL  1999
 9  Acura 2.3CL/3.0CL  1999
10  Acura       2.5TL  1995
# ... with 39,260 more rows
```

So far, I've performed two operations on the original fuel economy data. First, I selected the columns relevant to the vehicle product information. Then I arranged the rows by make, model, and year. Conducting these steps required two separate chunks of code and two separate variables. The following is what the code looks like so far:

```
## select the product info from the car
vehicles.product <- as_tibble(
   select(vehicles,make,model,year)
)

## arrange the rows of the vehicle product data
vehicles.product.arranged <- as.tibble(
   arrange(vehicles.product,make,model,year)
)
```

This may seem fairly legible, but when there are several consecutive processing steps the code can become quite hard to follow. In the following section, I will introduce a new syntax for chaining operations together to make the larger amounts of code more legible.

# Chaining operations together

Part of the expressive power of `dplyr` comes from its ability to chain data processing operations one after the other. The `%>%` symbol can be used with `dplyr` functions to chain together operations. The way it works is that the result of all of the expression before the `%>%` symbol is used as the first argument of the function that comes after the `%>%` symbol. In the following demonstration, I use the `%>%` symbol to put together the `select` and `arrange` operations:

```
vehicles.product.arranged <- as_tibble(
  vehicles %>% ## start with the original data
  select(make,model,year,cylinders) %>% ## select the columns
  arrange(make,model,year) ## arrange the rows
)
```

The previous chain of operations starts with the `vehicles` dataframe containing the original data. The `vehicles` dataframe is then followed by the `%>%` symbol, so it is passed as the first argument to the following function, which is the `select()` function. As such, the first argument of the `select()` function does not need to be specified, because the function comes after the `%>%` symbol. The `select()` function then returns a dataframe that becomes the first argument to the `arrange()` function. The output of the `arrange()` function is the result of the overall expression.

In this way, it is possible to express a series of transformations much more cohesively. As data processing steps add up, the `%>%` operator can go a long way to make code more manageable.

Another very useful feature `dplyr` is the ability to filter the rows of a dataframe based on their values. In the following section, I will introduce the `filter()` function of the `dplyr` package.

# Filtering the rows of a dataframe

You can `filter` rows as a function of the content of a row using the `filter()` function. (Recall from the previous chapters that you used filtering steps to remove outliers and `NA` values.)

In the `filter()` function, each of the arguments following the first is what the documentation refers to as a *logical predicate*. In other words, each of the arguments are assertions that some logical expression should be true.

The logical expressions used for filtering are defined in terms of the column names of the input dataframe. Here are some possible examples of logical predicates that could be used as arguments to the `filter()` function:

- `column.name > 6`
- `column.name == "abc"`
- `!is.na( column.name )`

A good application of the `filter()` function to the fuel economy dataset could be to find data for just one model. There is likely a lot of variation in the fuel economy data from model to model, so we could get a more consistent result by just focusing on one model.

In the following continuation of `dplyr_intro.R`, all of rows corresponding to the `Toyota Camry` model are selected from the original dataset using the `filter()` function. To keep the printout neat, the only the make, model, and year columns are selected for now:

```
## filter data to just the toyota camry
vehicles.camry <- as.tibble(
  car_data %>%
  filter(
    make == "Toyota",
    model=="Camry"
  ) %>%
  select(make,model,year)
)
print(vehicles.camry)
```

Printing the filtered data will reveal a list of entries, where the make and model are `Toyota` and `Camry` respectively:

```
> print(vehicles.camry)
# A tibble: 125 x 3
       make  model  year
      <fctr> <fctr> <int>
 1 Toyota  Camry  1993
 2 Toyota  Camry  1993
 3 Toyota  Camry  1993
 4 Toyota  Camry  1993
 5 Toyota  Camry  1994
 6 Toyota  Camry  1994
 7 Toyota  Camry  1994
 8 Toyota  Camry  1995
 9 Toyota  Camry  1995
10 Toyota  Camry  1995
# ... with 115 more rows
>
```

Not surprisingly, there are multiple entries for each `make`, `model`, and `year`; likely due to different sizes, trims, engines, and so on. In order to get a general sense of how the fuel economy changes year to year, one possible approach is to find the average fuel economy across all of the variations of `Camry` by year. This isn't a very accurate measure, since it does not account for the number of sales of each variation, but it may be enough to see a general trend which is worth exploring further.

In the next section, I will show how to use the `group_by()` and `summarize()` functions together in order to create a new dataframe that summarizes the data by group. In particular, the `group_by()` and `summarize()` functions used together will allow you to create a new dataframe with the yearly average fuel consumption across all of the `Toyota Camry` variations.

# Summarizing data by category

The `summarize()` function reduces the columns of a dataframe to a summary. The arguments to the `summarize()` function are expressions which create new variables a function of the rows of other columns. Here are a couple examples of possible arguments to the `summarize()` function:

- `avg.column.1 = mean(column.1)`
- `sum.column.2 = sum(column.2)`

The `group_by()` function causes all of the subsequent operations to be performed *by group*. The arguments to the `group_by()` function are the names of columns that the result should be grouped by. When the `group_by()` function is followed by the `summarize()` function, the summary is applied to each unique group.

The best way to understand the `group_by()` function is with a demonstration. In the following continuation of `dplyr_intro.R`, the fuel economy data is grouped by year and summarized by the mean value of `barrels08`. Additionally, the `filter()` function is used to `filter` the data to include only `Toyota Camry` models.

The `barrels08` column is an estimate of the annual fuel consumption. In the external resources I've included a link to the reference for the data variables in the fuel economy dataset.

```
### find the average fuel consumption by year:
camry.fuel_economy.by_year <- as_tibble(
  vehicles %>%
  group_by(year) %>%
  filter(
    make=="Toyota",
    model=="Camry"
  ) %>%
  summarize(
    avg.annual.consumption = mean(barrels08)
  )
)
print(camry.fuel_economy.by_year)
```

The result is a dataframe containing two columns. The first of these columns is called `year`. The `year` column is the result of the `year` parameter passed to the `group_by()` function, which caused the `summarize()` function to create a summary of the data for each year. Each row of data represents an individual year.

The second column, `avg.annual.consumption`, is a result of the expression in the `summarize()` function, which assigns the `mean` of the `barrels08` column to the `avg.annual.consumption` variable. Each row in the data corresponds to a single year and contains the mean value of `barrels08` for all variations in the corresponding year.

The following is what the `camry.fuel_economy.by_year` dataframe looks like when it is printed:

```
> print(camry.fuel_economy.by_year)
# A tibble: 35 x 2
     year avg.annual.consumption
    <int>                  <dbl>
1    1984               12.34269
2    1985               13.01336
3    1986               12.85699
4    1987               13.20553
5    1988               15.08234
6    1989               15.16997
7    1990               15.28812
8    1991               15.22018
9    1992               16.07121
10   1993               16.58439
# ... with 25 more rows
>
```

In the following continuation of `dplyr_intro.R`, the `plot()` function is used in order to visualize the data. The type=l parameter is specified in the call to the plot function to indicate that it should be a line plot.

```
plot(camry.fuel_economy.by_year,type='l')
```

Plotting the data shows an upward trend in annual vehicle fuel consumption from about 1985 to 1995, and a downward trend in annual vehicle fuel consumption from about 1995 to the present. This trend is the average across all Toyota Camry variations.

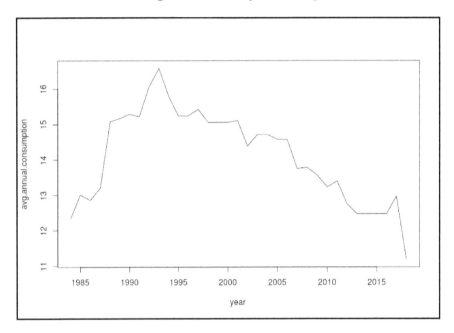

Next, let's compare the Camry fuel efficiency to the gas prices in USD over the same time period to see if there might be a relationship between fuel economy and gas prices. First, at the beginning of the `dplyr_intro.R` script, the `gas_prices.csv` dataset is read to an R dataframe as follows:

```
gas_prices <- read.csv("data/gas_prices.csv")
```

The next task is to get the gas price by year over the same time period as the fuel economy data. Because the data is given by year and month, the maximum fuel price for each year should be sufficient to show the general trend. The Camry fuel economy data begins in 1984, so the gas price data should be filtered so that it is from 1984 to the present. In the following continuation of dplyr_intro.R the group_by() function, the filter() function, and the summarize() function are used to get the maximum gas prices for each year:

```
gas_prices.by_year <- as.tibble(
  gas_prices %>%
  group_by(year) %>%
  select(year,value) %>%
  filter(year>=1984) %>%
  summarize(
    max_price = max(value)
  )
)
```

The result is a dataframe with a year column and a max_price column:

```
> print(gas_prices.by_year)
# A tibble: 34 x 2
      year max_price
     <int>     <dbl>
 1   1984     1.526
 2   1985     1.471
 3   1986     1.468
 4   1987     1.302
 5   1988     1.317
 6   1989     1.411
 7   1990     1.734
 8   1991     1.638
 9   1992     1.511
10   1993     1.498
# ... with 24 more rows
```

Finally, the gas_prices.by_year dataframe is visualized using a line plot in the same way that as the fuel economy:

```
plot(gas_prices.by_year,type='l')
```

Plotting the gas price data shows an upward trend starting at around 1995; about the time that the average fuel economy of the Toyota Camry started its downward trend:

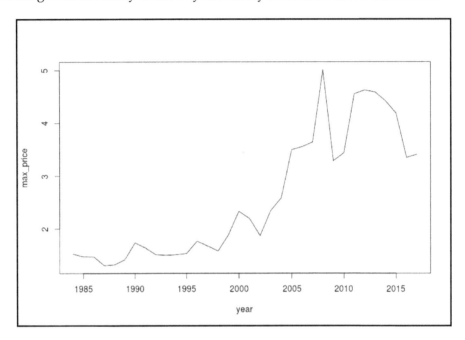

This isn't really a significant finding in and of itself because the vehicle fuel economy data does not account for sales by model, and because correlation does not imply causation. However, the previous demonstration shows the power of dplyr to easily manipulate datasets and draw insight. The dplyr package not only enables you to easily express a number of heavy processing steps, but it allows you to do so in a language that is easy to read and comprehend.

At this point, you should have everything you need to estimate the total road length in 2011 (the exercise from the previous chapter) using code that is more concise and easier to follow. In the following section, I will revisit the project one last time using the dplyr library.

# Rewriting code using dplyr

In the previous chapter, R was used to find the estimate of the total road length in 2011. Here are the steps that were completed in the previous chapter, written using dplyr verbs:

- Filter out the rows with a mean greater than 2000
- Filter out the rows in which all values are NA
- Mutate the 2011 column to create a copy in which the NA values are replaced with the row mean
- Select the new 2011 column and find the sum of its values

At the beginning of dplyr_intro.R, the first step should be to read artificial_roads_by_region.csv to an R dataframe as follows:

```
roads.lengths <- read.csv("data/artificial_roads_by_region.csv")
```

Next, In the following continuation of dplyr_intro.R, a copy of the original roads length data called roads.length2 is created. The row averages and the row sums of the roads.length2 dataframe are calculated and added as columns to the dataframe. These columns will help with the filtering steps.

```
roads.lengths2<-roads.lengths
roads.lengths2$mean_val <- rowMeans(
  roads.lengths[,-1],
  na.rm = TRUE
)
roads.lengths2$row_total<-rowSums(
  roads.lengths[,-1],
  na.rm=TRUE
)
```

Putting all of the steps together using dplyr functions, in the following continuation of dplyr_intro.R, the 2011 road length estimate is calculated:

```
roads.2011.estimate <-
  roads.lengths2 %>%
    filter(
      mean_val<2000,
      row_total>0
    ) %>%
    mutate(
      X2011.new=ifelse(
      is.na(X2011),
      mean_val,
      X2011
```

```
    )
  ) %>%
  select(
    X2011.new
  )
print(sum(roads.2011.estimate))
```

The result is `808648.3`, the same as in the previous chapter!

# Summary

In summary, the `dplyr` package builds on the R language to make an even more expressive and concise language for data manipulation. In this chapter, the estimate for the total road length in `2011` is the same as in the previous chapter, but the code used to get there is more concise and easier to follow. This can mean less time spent on navigating numerous processing steps and variable names, and more time spent organizing the data.

This concludes the second section of this book, which dealt with a more formulated approach to data wrangling. If you've read up to this point, congratulations! You now have a broad understanding of the tools, approaches, and skills involved in manipulating data.

In the remaining part of the book, I will discuss advanced methods for retrieving and storing data. First, large sources of data are often made available through web interfaces called **APIs**. I will discuss how to use APIs to retrieve data in the next chapter.

Second, working with large amounts of data is sometimes made easier with the use of databases. In `Chapter 9`, *Working with Large Datasets*, I will introduce databases and show you how they can be used to store and quickly retrieve large amounts of data.

# 8
# Getting Data from the Web

It is convenient to contain and distribute small amounts of data using static files. Files work well for sources of data that are low volume, self contained, and infrequently updated. Many sources of data, however, are a part of massive web applications or data archives that are updated constantly. Sources, such as Wikipedia and Seeclickfix, that store data in large databases will often make their data available through **APIs** (**application programming interfaces**) that allow users to retrieve small selections of the data. In fact, the Seeclickfix and Wikipedia datasets used in previous chapters were obtained using APIs.

In this chapter, I will walk through the steps of using Python to retrieve the data from the Seeclickfix API. This chapter will include the following sections:

- Logistical overview
- Introducing APIs
- Using Python to retrieve data from APIs
- Using URL parameters to filter the results

## Logistical overview

In this chapter, I will do a demonstration of the steps used to retrieve Seeclickfix data from the Seeclickfix API. While the resulting datasets are not exactly the same as those used in the previous chapters, they are quite similar. In this chapter, I will demonstrate two Python programs. The first, `get_recent_issues.py`, is used to access the Seeclickfix API from Python, retrieve data, and output a JSON file with the data.

The second script, `get_scf_date_range.py`, is used to retrieve data from the issue reports that occurred on the first day of January 2017. The `get_scf_date_range.py` script will output a CSV file with the data.

This chapter will be different from the other chapters in a couple of ways. First, because the data for the chapter is retrieved over the internet as a part of the demonstrations, there are no input data files that are used with the demonstrations.

Second, because APIs are outside of my control, and subject to change, I've made a version of this chapter available online that can be updated as needed. The link to online version of the chapter is made available in the *Links and Further Reading* document in the external resources.

All of the external resources for this book are available at the following link: `https://goo.gl/8S58ra`.

# Filesystem setup

For this chapter, there is no input data, however, there are output data files. For this chapter, you should create a project folder containing an `output_data` folder to contain the output data. The setup that I will use is as follows:

```
chapter8/
-->get_recent_issues.py
-->get_scf_date_range.py
---->output_data/
```

# Installing the requests module

For this chapter, you will need the Python requests module. I've included installation instructions for the requests module in the Installation document in the external resources.

# Internet connection

Another difference between this chapter and the others is that the Python scripts used in this chapter retrieve data over the internet. In order for the Python scripts to work properly, you will need a stable internet connection while they are running.

# Introducing APIs

Most communication over the web is done using `http` protocol, which specifies a set of request/response protocols for exchanging data between a *client* and a *server*. The client, which is often a web browser, submits a request for data from the server, and the server sends a response. Typically, the response is an HTML web page. The response, however, can also be data in some text format.

The most popular types of requests are `get` requests and `post` requests. In this chapter, I will just cover `get` requests, which will be used to retrieve data from the API. A `get` request is a request that asks for data from the server.

An **API** specifies a URL and a set of variables that can be used to retrieve data using `http` requests. The following is the URL where the Seeclickfix API is located: `https://Seeclickfix.com/api/v2`.

When you go to the Seeclickfix API URL in a web browser, or to any website for that matter, the web browser submits a `get` request to the URL. If the `get` request is successful, the web browser will display the response, which is usually a web page. When you go to the base URL of the API, you will notice that the result is not a web page, but rather a collection of JSON data:

The JSON data here isn't that important, but it's worth noting that the response from the server is in JSON format. This will make it possible to easily retrieve and process the data from the API.

In order to retrieve actual data from the API, you will need to be a bit more specific. The Seeclickfix API is divided by resource. In addition to data on issue reports, the Seeclickfix API also has data relating to geographic regions and users of the platform. The reason I know this is that the Seeclickfix API, like most APIs, makes documentation available. The documentation describes in detail the API and its usage. The Seeclickfix API documentation website is available at `http://dev.seeclickfix.com/`.

On the right side of the main documentation page is a panel listing more specific sections of the documentation, including a section for issues:

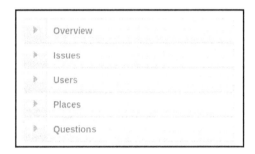

I would encourage you to look explore the documentation for the Seeclickfix API and other APIs to get a sense for how they are set up. For now I will just go straight to the page for issues since that is the resource that I am looking for. This brings me to `http://dev.seeclickfix.com/v2/issues/`, where at the top of the page is a URL for listing issue reports:

The previous notation means that submitting a `get` request to the URL will return a list of *issues*. Recall that navigating to a URL in a browser causes the browser to submit a `get` request to the server at that URL. In order to test out the URL, try going to `https://seeclickfix.com/api/v2/issues` in a browser. Doing so should now reveal a JSON dataset containing a list of issues:

←  C  ⌂  🔒 Secure | https://**seeclickfix.com**/api/v2/issues

{"metadata":{"pagination":{"entries":443532,"page":1,"per_page":20,"pages":22177,"next
page=2,"previous_page":null,"previous_page_url":null}},"issues":[{"id":3847850,"statu
operate early in the mornings of weekends causing nuisance to the neighborhood. Please
in weekends.","rating":1,"lat":40.7133505251267,"lng":-74.0351940064698,"address":"Lib
11-04T06:49:39-04:00","acknowledged_at":null,"closed_at":null,"reopened_at":null,"upda
04:00","shortened_url":null,"url":"https://seeclickfix.com/api/v2/issues/3847850","poi
[-74.03519400646978,40.71335052512671]},"html_url":"https://seeclickfix.com/issues/384
Collection","organization":"City of Jersey
City","url":"https://seeclickfix.com/api/v2/request_types/16281","related_issues_url":
lat=40.7133505251267&lng=-74.0351940064698&request_types=16281&sort=distance"},"commen
:"https://seeclickfix.com/api/v2/issues/3847850/flag","transitions":{"close_url":"http
{"id":1488079,"name":"Stefano","witty_title":"Civic Crusader","avatar":{"full":"https:
5e06fcc664c6376bbf654cbd67df857ff81918c5f5c6a2345226093147382de9.png","square_100x100"
5e06fcc664c6376bbf654cbd67df857ff81918c5f5c6a2345226093147382de9.png"},"role":"Registe
{"video_url":null,"image_full":null,"image_square_100x100":null,"representative_image
f6b4bb46a308421d38fc042b1a74691fe7778de981d59493fa89297f6caa86a1.png"}},{"id":3847804,
is a large crack on the side of the cart.  Items cannot come out, but water/bugs can p
","rating":1,"lat":35.0623003,"lng":-78.9127579,"address":"212 Woodrow Street Fayettev
04:00","acknowledged_at":"2017-11-04T06:28:04-04:00","closed_at":null,"reopened_at":nu
04:00","shortened_url":null,"url":"https://seeclickfix.com/api/v2/issues/3847804","poi
[-78.9127579,35.0623003]},"html_url":"https://seeclickfix.com/issues/3847804","request
- Service Request","url":"https://seeclickfix.com/api/v2/request_types/7589","related_
lat=35.0623003&lng=-78.9127579&request_types=7589&sort=distance"},"comment_url":"https
clickfix.com/api/v2/issues/3847804/flag","transitions":{},"reporter":{"id":0,"name":"A
{"full":"https://seeclickfix.com/anonymous-avatar-150x150.png","square_100x100":"https
127a80e459a3fd9874ad8556fb9140ffa2f046dec0dbebe1ff67e922098c8c02.png"},"role":"Registe
{"video_url":null,"image_full":null,"image_square_100x100":null,"representative_image_
f2af6312d3b7cdc128b1c472da1e696af6827f90d98d4aedb5eb55d9f575537f.png"}},{"id":3847803,
Property","description":"Dead baby deer. If your coming from McGinnis Ferry it's Just
right side of the road. ","rating":1,"lat":34.0457402859076,"lng":-84.1418908461992,"a
04:00","acknowledged_at":null,"closed_at":null,"reopened_at":null,"updated_at":"2017-1
04:00","shortened_url":null,"url":"https://seeclickfix.com/api/v2/issues/3847803","poi
[-84.1418908461992,34.045740285907601]},"html_url":"https://seeclickfix.com/issues/3847
Property","organization":"City of Johns
Creek","url":"https://seeclickfix.com/api/v2/request_types/6815","related_issues_url":
lat=34.0457402859076&lng=-84.1418908461992&request_types=6815&sort=distance"},"comment
"https://seeclickfix.com/api/v2/issues/3847803/flag","transitions":{"close_url":"https
{"id":1486790,"name":"Kathy","witty_title":"Civic Pride","avatar":
{"full":"https://seeclickfix.com/files/user_images/0003/3782/IMG_2630.JPG","square_100
.JPG"},"role":"Registered User","civic_points":250},"media":
{"video_url":null,"image_full":null,"image_square_100x100":null,"representative_image_
f440c460c081633aa0c37615138587a0c1e11381e099cd48e0bc92c0babfe984.png"}},{"id":3847802,
4mins early than app showed\n\n--------------------\nservice_date=11-04-2017;\nagency

At this point, it is possible to copy and paste the data into a JSON file, or, in most browsers, to save the page as a JSON file directly. In the next section though, I will show how Python can be used to retrieve data from the API and store the data in a JSON file. Eventually, I will demonstrate how working within Python allows you to go a step further to retrieve more custom data selections.

# Using Python to retrieve data from APIs

The first step is to import the `requests` module. I will also import the `json` module, which can be used to output the data retrieved from the API to a JSON file. In the beginning of `get_recent_issues.py`, the following code imports the `requests` and `json` modules:

```
import requests
import json
```

The next step is to create a string called **base URL**. The base URL is the beginning part of the URL, and can be followed by additional parameters. For now, the base URL is all you need, but in the next section you will build on it in order get data iteratively. In the following continuation of `get_recent_issues.py`, a string is created containing the base URL for the *issues* resource of the Seeclickfix API:

```
import requests
import json

## build a base url which is the endpoint to the api
## for this script, this is all you need
base_url = "https://seeclickfix.com/api/v2/issues?"
```

The next step is to replicate the action of the browser. In other words, you will need to submit a `get` request to the URL and store the response. This can be done using the `requests.get()` function of the `requests` module, which takes as an argument a URL string and returns a `response` object containing the information in the response from the server. In the following continuation of `get_recent_issues.py`, the `requests` module is used to submit a `get` request to the base URL:

```
....
base_url = "https://seeclickfix.com/api/v2/issues?"

## submit a get request to the URL and
## collect the response in the response object
response = requests.get(base_url)
```

An `http` response contains additional information besides the main content. The requests module parses the response into its various components. Because the body of this particular response is expected to be in JSON format, you can use the `response.json()` function of a `response` object to both extract the JSON text, and parse the text into a Python data structure.

At this point, it may be worth doing a bit of exploration of the data in the response, though I will simply save the result to a file for now. In the following continuation of `get_recent_issues.py`, the `response.json()` method is used to extract the response body, which is then saved to a JSON file:

```
response = requests.get(base_url)

## use the json module to write the response data
## from the api into a json file
fout = open("output_data/scf_recent_issues.json","w")
json.dump(response.json(),fout,indent=4)
fout.close()
```

Running `get_recent_issues.py` should now produce an output JSON file containing the 10 most recent issues reported on the Seeclickfix platform:

This covers how to get data within Python, but it does not take advantage of the programming interface that Python offers. In the next section, I will demonstrate the use of URL parameters to retrieve larger and more specific collections of data.

# Using URL parameters to filter the results

In this section, I will retrieve all of the issue reports from the Seeclickfix API that occurred on the first day of January 2017. To start with, I will create a new file called `get_scf_date_range.py`, and import the `requests` module and the `csv` as follows:

```
import requests
import csv
```

The goal will be to gather all of the issue reports that occur during the first day of January 2017 and to store the results in a CSV file. In order to do this, you will need to make use of **URL parameters**. URL parameters are custom values that are added on to the end of a URL to further specify the get request.

The Seeclickfix API documentation on the *issues* resource shows a number of URL parameters that can be used. After looking through the Seeclickfix API documentation at `http://dev.seeclickfix.com/v2/issues/`, you may identify three particular parameters that are of use. The first two of these are the `after` and `before` parameters:

- **after**= `:time` - must be a timestamp in ISO 8601 format: YYYY-MM-DDTHH:MM:SSZ

- **before**= `:time` - must be a timestamp in ISO 8601 format: YYYY-MM-DDTHH:MM:SSZ

These parameters can be used to specify that the results should be after January 01, 2017 and before January 02, 2017. URL parameters are specified after a base URL using the following syntax:

```
<url>?<parameter1>=<value1>&<parameter2>=<value2>
```

In the following continuation of `get_scf_date_range.py`, the URL parameters are added to the URL string to restrict the results so that they only contain data for the first date of January 2017:

```
import requests
import csv

url = "https://seeclickfix.com/api/v2/issues?"

## restrict the result to issues after January 2017
url+="after=2017-01-01T00:00:00"

## restrict the result to issues before February 2017
url+="&before=2017-01-02T00:00:00"
```

The third parameter that will be of use is the `page` parameter:

> • **page=** `:page_number` - number of the page to return, default: 1

The `page` parameter allows you to get data that is beyond the initial set of results, in the following continuation of `get_scf_date_range.py`, I've added the `page` parameter to the URL string, but left it blank:

```
. . . .
url+="&before=2017-01-02T00:00:00"

## leave the page parameter empty so that it
## can be dynamically changed
url+="&page="
```

Rather than specifying just one page for the `page` parameter, the strategy I will use is to make a number of repetitive `get` requests, each containing a subsequent page number. This way, it is possible to get multiple pages of the data instead of just one.

However, before conducting the `get` requests, I will do some initial setup, creating the output file and specifying data variables to be extracted. In the following continuation of `get_scf_date_range.py`, an array of column headers is created. These column headers will also be used as keys to extract the desired data variables from the original data retrieved from the API. A new output file is then opened and used to create a `writer` object. The column headers are then written to the first row of the output file:

```
. . . .
url+="&page="
```

```
## create a list of field names that should be extracted
fields=["created_at","closed_at","summary","address"]

## open the output file and create a writer
## write the column headers to the output file
fout = open("output_data/scf_date_range_issues.csv","w")
writer=csv.writer(fout)
writer.writerow(fields)

fout.close()
```

The next step is to perform the `get` requests, page by page. To set up this process, in the following continuation of `get_scf_date_range.py`, I will first create a variable called `page` to contain the page number, and a variable called `data` containing the extracted data from the `http` response:

```
. . . .
writer.writerow(fields)

## initialize the page and data variables
page=1
data=requests.get(base_url+str(page)).json()["issues"]

fout.close()
```

 The next bit of code will require a Python tool that hasn't been covered yet in this book, the **while loop**. A while loop works like a for loop, except it runs continuously until a certain condition is met. The condition is specified in the clause header of the while loop.

You can read about while loops in the Python documentation at the following link:

```
https://docs.python.org/3/reference/compound_stmts.html#while
```

Next, in the following continuation of `get_scf_date_range.py`, a `while` loop is created to continuously increase the page number and submit `get` requests until there is no more data left. If there is data, each data entry is converted to an array and written to the output CSV file:

```
. . . .
data=requests.get(base_url+str(page)).json()["issues"]

## go page by page until there is no data
while len(data)>0:
    ## if there is data, iterate over the
    ## data entries, writing the result to the output
```

```
for entry in data:
    row=[]
    for field in fields:
        row.append(entry[field])
    writer.writerow(row)

## in each iteration of the loop,
## increase the page number and get
## the data for the subsequent page
page+=1
data=requests.get(base_url+str(page)).json()["issues"]
```

```
fout.close()
```

Now, running `get_scf_date_range.py` will produce a CSV dataset containing information on all of the issue reports in the first day of 2017:

| | A created_at | B closed_at | summary |
|---|---|---|---|
| 2 | 2017-01-01T18:46:35-05:00 | | Post to neighbors |
| 3 | 2017-01-01T18:28:12-05:00 | | Illegal Dumping |
| 4 | 2017-01-01T18:07:41-05:00 | | Shoes on Wire |
| 5 | 2017-01-01T17:55:57-05:00 | | Street Light Repair |
| 6 | 2017-01-01T17:49:45-05:00 | | Illegal Dumping |
| 7 | 2017-01-01T17:49:36-05:00 | | Illegal Dumping |
| 8 | 2017-01-01T17:47:11-05:00 | | Bike Share Station Lo |
| 9 | 2017-01-01T17:41:06-05:00 | | Pile of scrap wood |
| 10 | 2017-01-01T17:38:38-05:00 | | Yard and/or Structure |
| 11 | 2017-01-01T17:11:32-05:00 | | Park Maintenance |
| 12 | 2017-01-01T16:59:20-05:00 | | Graffiti Removal |
| 13 | 2017-01-01T16:57:48-05:00 | | Yard and/or Structure |
| 14 | 2017-01-01T16:56:54-05:00 | | Graffiti Removal |
| 15 | 2017-01-01T16:52:33-05:00 | | Illegal Dumping |
| 16 | 2017-01-01T16:43:40-05:00 | | Sign Missing Investiga |
| 17 | 2017-01-01T16:30:10-05:00 | | Street and Sidewalk Is |
| 18 | 2017-01-01T16:22:27-05:00 | | Street and Sidewalk Is |
| 19 | 2017-01-01T16:18:46-05:00 | | Graffiti Removal |
| 20 | 2017-01-01T16:15:44-05:00 | | Manhole Cover Issue |
| 21 | 2017-01-01T16:15:23-05:00 | | Manhole Cover Issue |
| 22 | 2017-01-01T16:11:18-05:00 | | Street and Sidewalk Is |
| 23 | 2017-01-01T16:07:47-05:00 | | Signs / Bus Shelters / |
| 24 | 2017-01-01T16:01:29-05:00 | | Code Enforcement |
| 25 | 2017-01-01T15:59:07-05:00 | | Code Enforcement |
| 26 | 2017-01-01T15:56:43-05:00 | | Other: Drainage / Floo |
| 27 | 2017-01-01T15:39:08-05:00 | | Rear junk |

# Summary

In summary, APIs are an excellent way of retrieving data that is otherwise hard to get, and being able to work with APIs gives you access to a large range of datasets, particularly when working from within a programming language such as Python. This chapter was about retrieving data from particularly large data sources.

The next chapter will be about processing particularly large data files. When processing data files that are larger than a certain size, there are a few things to take into consideration. In the next (and final) chapter, I discuss how to use databases to store large datasets and how to manage memory while processing them.

# 9
# Working with Large Datasets

All of the approaches to data wrangling that have been covered in this book are good for processing datasets that are sufficiently small. Once datasets reach a certain size, however, a different approach may be required. For even larger collections of data, data mining techniques may be more appropriate.

In this chapter, I will discuss the approaches to working with datasets that are not too big to be processed on a single computer, but are too big to be read into memory all at once. I will discuss computer memory and introduce databases as a means of storing data. This chapter will include the following sections:

- Logistical Overview
- Understanding computer memory
- Understanding databases
- Introducing MongoDB
- Interfacing with MongoDB from Python

## Logistical overview

This chapter will include two demonstrations. The first of these will show you how to import data into the MongoDB database and how to update the data. This will not require any code files, but it will require some setup, which is detailed in the following subsections.

The second demonstration will show you how to interface with MongoDB from within Python, and using a Python script called `process_large_data.py`. The finished code is available in the `code` folder of the external resources.

All of the external resources are available at the following link: `https://goo.gl/8S58ra`.

# System requirements

To follow along with the exercises, you should have at least 25 GB of disk space free. If disk space is a limiting factor, you can still follow along using a smaller version of the dataset, as I will explain in the next section.

# Data

To demonstrate working with large datasets, I've created an artificial dataset, `fake_weather_data.csv`, containing fake weather data since 1980. The dataset is indeed quite large (4 GB), and importing the data into a database will take up even more memory. If you are limited by disk space or do not want to wait for the data to be processed, you may alternatively use a smaller version of the dataset called `fake_weather_data_small.csv` along with the demonstrations. If you use the smaller dataset, be sure to change the filename in the demonstrations accordingly.

The data for this chapter is available in the `data` folder of the external resources.

# File system setup

For this chapter, there should be just one project folder containing `process_large_data.py`, the Python code for the second demonstration. The project folder should also contain a data folder containing the *Chapter 9* dataset.

# Installing MongoDB

To follow along with the demonstrations in this chapter, you will need to install and set up MongoDB. You will need both the database and the server installed, and you will need to have an instance of the server running on your computer.

For `process_large_data.py`, you will also need to install `pymongo`, a Python module for interfacing with MongoDB.

Links and guidelines for installation are available in the *Installation* document in the external resources.

# Planning out your time

Several of the activities in this chapter will take quite some time, so as you follow along with the demonstrations, be prepared to do something else while you wait for certain processes to complete.

# Cleaning up

Lastly, if you use the larger dataset, you will end up using a lot of memory on your system (20 GB or more). Be sure to delete the data and databases when you are done if you would like to free up the disk space. Additionally, in the installation instructions for MongoDB I've also included instructions to shut down the MongoDB server when you are done.

# Understanding computer memory

To make sense of why processing large files requires a new approach, I will briefly discuss computer memory and databases here. Feel free to skip ahead if you are familiar with how memory and databases work.

In computer hardware, **memory** is the medium that stores data, programs, and files. The hardware for computer memory is split into **primary storage**, which generally takes the form of **RAM** (random access memory), and **secondary storage**, which generally takes the form of a **hard drive**. Primary storage is used for storing the machine code and the data of active programs, while secondary storage is used for storing all data and files not currently in use. This division in memory usage reflects a few differences in the hardware used for each.

The first difference is that RAM (used for primary storage) is cleared when the computer is shut down, while data stored on hard drives (used for secondary storage) persists. The second difference is that data stored on RAM is much faster to access and modify then data stored on a hard disk. The third difference, which follows on from the second, is that RAM is more expensive per unit of storage capacity. Because RAM is more expensive, it is likely that significantly more data can fit on your computer's hard drive then on your computer's active memory. (This may not necessarily be the case for some computers which rely on cloud storage.)

When a computer program is run, the program lives in the computer's RAM along with all of the data that it uses. When a collection of data is not in use, it lives on the computer's hard drive. Because the RAM available to a computer is limited, so is the amount of data that a computer program can use at once. Most operating systems don't limit the amount of memory that a program can use, so reading too much data will usually cause your computer to crash. This is why there is a limit to the amount of data that can be processed at once.

Most operating systems have an interface to monitor RAM usage. The following is my computer's memory monitor:

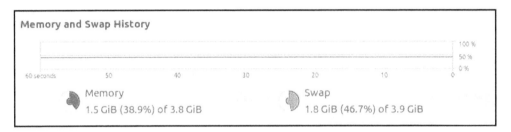

My computer is fairly old, so I have 4 GB of RAM (that was a lot at the time I bought it). At the time of writing this, 4 GB to 16 GB seems to be the general range for RAM on newer laptops. When I took the previous screenshot of my computer's memory monitor, I was using about 39% of the RAM (taken up by some browser tabs).

 The green line (**Swap**) represents some additional space allocated on the hard drive that can be used in case the RAM gets full. This is a Linux feature that can be helpful, but I won't cover it here since it is specific to Linux.

The dataset for this chapter is about 4 GB large, so even if I weren't already using 39% of the RAM, there wouldn't be enough space to read all of the data. Data takes more memory when used by a program than when it is stored in a static file. This is because it is represented by a data structure and not just by text.

To demonstrate how a program can use up RAM, I've created a program, available in the external resources, called dont_do_this.py. As the name would suggest, you should not run the program on your computer (or you should do so at your own risk). The dont_do_this.py program reads data line by line and appends each row to a Python list. The Python list called myData grows either until the program completes or until there is no more RAM left available on the computer, causing the computer to crash. The following is the code for dont_do_this.py:

```
## this may crash your computer,
## so use this code for demonstration purposes,
## or run at your own risk (without any unsaved work open)

import csv
myData=[]

fin = open('data/fake_weather_data.csv','r',newline='')
reader = csv.reader(fin)
for row in reader:
    myData.append(row)
```

When I run dont_do_this.py on my computer, the RAM usage quickly ramps up as the Python program collects more and more of the data. I took the following screenshot of the memory monitor after running the program for about a minute:

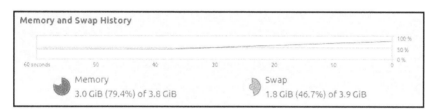

If I had left the program running, it would have crashed the computer in another minute or so. After cancelling the program, the RAM usage quickly drops back to around 40%, as the following screenshot shows:

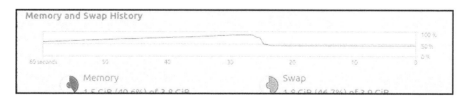

The point here is that data uses memory, and there is a limited amount of it. Rather than reading in a whole data file, sufficiently large datasets should be processed line by line so that they does not use all of the computer's memory.

# Understanding databases

In addition to using plenty of memory, large amounts of data can also take a long time to process. In some cases, it may make sense to process a large dataset from one input file to another output file. Data wrangling, however, is often an iterative process, involving back and forth between data analysis and modification. It can be hard to iterate with a large dataset using a Python script. This is where **database management systems** can be helpful.

A **database** simply refers to an organized collection of data. In contrast to files, databases are typically organized structurally to index each of the **documents** (another word for data entry) making it faster to retrieve specific documents or groups of documents. A database management system is software for interfacing with a database to do the following:

- Retrieve data from a database
- Modify data in a database
- Write data to a database

Database management systems define a language for analyzing and modifying data that does not require you to read all of the data into memory at once, or to write a separate program. This can make database management systems an excellent tool for working with large datasets. In the next section, I will introduce a database management system called MongoDB and do a basic demonstration of some of its features.

# Introducing MongoDB

MongoDB is what is referred to as a **NoSQL** database, which refers to a data model that is not tabular, as opposed to **relational** databases which are tabular. The structure of data in MongoDB is analogous to JSON, with each of the documents consisting of key-value pairs.

Once you have MongoDB set up on your computer and you have the MongoDB server running, you can import your data into a database using the `mongoimport` terminal command. The `mongoimport` command will take data from a static file, parse the data, and place the data into a database. The documentation for `mongoimport` is available at the following link: `https://docs.mongodb.com/manual/reference/program/mongoimport/`.

There are a few parameters that need to be specified along with the `mongoimport` command. The first of these is the name of the input file which should be written after the `--file` parameter. The command should be run in a terminal from the directory containing `fake_weather_data.csv`, so the filename is specified by the following:

```
$ mongoimport --file fake_weather_data.csv
```

Next, since you are importing data from a CSV file, you will need to specify `--type csv` in order to indicate a CSV file. In addition, the `--headerline` parameter should be specified to indicate that the field names to be used are those specified in the first line of the CSV file.

Lastly, documents in MongoDB are organized under two levels:

- MongoDB documents belong to a `collection` within MongoDB
- MongoDB `collections` belong to a `database`

As such, you will need to specify a name for the database with the `--database` parameter and a name for the collection with the `--collection` parameter. I will use `weather` for the database name and `records` for the collection name.

The following is the finished command to import the CSV data into MongoDB. Note that the import will take some time to complete (possibly a few hours depending on your system), so you may want to do something else for a little while while it finishes. Also note that you will need plenty of available storage on your hard drive (15 or so GB) in order to complete the import:

```
$ mongoimport --file fake_weather_data.csv --type csv --headerline --db
weather --collection records
```

Once the import is finished, the data is stored in the computer's hard drive in a database file that can be interfaced using MongoDB. To use MongoDB, you can enter a `mongo` shell from the terminal by entering the following command:

```
$ mongo
```

Inside the Mongo shell, you can write commands to interact directly with the database. To start with, you can use the following command to indicate the database which you would like to interact with:

```
> use weather
```

After selecting the database, the following will count the number of documents in the records collection:

```
> db.records.count()
```

The following will retrieve and display a single document:

```
> db.records.findOne()
```

The following screenshot is the result of running the previous commands in the mongo shell on my computer:

```
> use weather
switched to db weather
> db.records.count()
94608000
> db.records.findOne()
{
        "_id" : ObjectId("5a001e38b4b746a7889b644a"),
        "date" : "1980-01-01 00:00:00",
        "temperature" : 2.429978875842491,
        "is_cloudy" : 1,
        "is_sunny" : 0
}
>
```

MongoDB has a powerful language for querying and modifying documents in a collection, so I've included a link to the MongoDB documentation in the external resources for further reading. Rather than attempt to cover everything here, I will do a simple demonstration to change is_cloudy and is_sunny from integers to logical data types.

It is possible to update multiple documents in a collection using the update() function. The first argument to the update() function is a filter that selects which data should be updated. Commands in MongoDB are written a bit like Python dictionaries. The simplest filter is one in which a particular field has a particular value, and is written as follows:

```
{<fieldname>:<value>}
```

In order to select all of the fields where is_sunny is 1, you can use the following as the first argument to the updateMany() function:

```
{ is_sunny : 1 }
```

The next argument to the update() function is a structure that specifies the update that should take place. This takes the following form:

```
{ <update operator> : { <field> : <value> } }
```

The update operator to set a new value is $set. The second argument, which specifies that the is_sunny field should be set to true, as follows:

```
{ $set : { is_sunny : true } }
```

A third argument should be passed to the update() function that specifies that the operation should update multiple documents and not just one. Putting it all together, the following command will change the values of the is_sunny field from 1 to true where the value was 1 to begin with:

```
> db.records.update( { is_sunny : 1}, { $set : { is_sunny : true} }, {
multi : true } )
```

This will also take some time to finish. When it does finish, however, you can verify that the value of is_sunny is either 0 or true by running db.records.find(). The following is the output on my computer:

```
2491, "is_cloudy" : 1, "is_sunny" : 0 }

136, "is_cloudy" : 0, "is_sunny" : 0 }
4306, "is_cloudy" : 1, "is_sunny" : true }
3997, "is_cloudy" : 1, "is_sunny" : true }
3853, "is_cloudy" : 1, "is_sunny" : true }
91754, "is_cloudy" : 0, "is_sunny" : 0 }
51694, "is_cloudy" : 0, "is_sunny" : true }
86484, "is_cloudy" : 0, "is_sunny" : true }
8906, "is_cloudy" : 1, "is_sunny" : true }
45535, "is_cloudy" : 1, "is_sunny" : 0 }
64791, "is_cloudy" : 1, "is_sunny" : 0 }
49577, "is_cloudy" : 0, "is_sunny" : true }
5621, "is_cloudy" : 0, "is_sunny" : true }
24433, "is_cloudy" : 1, "is_sunny" : true }
95258, "is_cloudy" : 0, "is_sunny" : true }
7857, "is_cloudy" : 1, "is_sunny" : 0 }
43853, "is_cloudy" : 1, "is_sunny" : true }
56436, "is_cloudy" : 0, "is_sunny" : true }
68617, "is_cloudy" : 0, "is_sunny" : 0 }
```

If you wanted to, you could easily repeat this step to change 0 to `false` for the `is_cloudy` and `is_sunny` fields. This step isn't really necessary, though, as it will just take more time. After you are done with the demonstration, and with any personal exploration, you can remove the data from the database by running the following:

```
> db.records.remove({})
```

While MongoDB is quite powerful, it does not have the full capability of a programming language. In the next section, I will demonstrate how to interface MongoDB with Python to achieve the same result. Using Python to import data to MongoDB gives you the ability to process data as it is placed in the database.

# Interfacing with MongoDB from Python

Python can connect to MongoDB using the `pymongo` module. To start off with, I will create a file called `process_large_data.py` and import the `pymongo` and `csv` modules. You will need to import both `pymongo` and `MongoClient` as I have done in the demonstration:

```
import csv
import pymongo
from pymongo import MongoClient
```

`MongoClient` takes care of establishing a connection and interfacing with the database system. The following steps in `process_large_data.py` will create an object assigned to the collection variable, which can be used to insert documents into the database:

```
....
from pymongo import MongoClient

## create a MongoClient object,
## used to connect and interface
## with mongodb
client = MongoClient()

## these two lines create a collection
## object which allows you to interface
## with a particular collection
db = client.weather
collection = db["records2"]
```

The only thing left to do now is to read the data line by line and insert each row as a record into the database. This is where the `csv` module becomes quite useful. Recall that the Python's `csv` module reads CSV data row by row and not all at once. This means that using the `csv` module, it is possible to process a CSV dataset without reading the entire dataset into memory.

In the following continuation of `process_large_data.py`, a CSV reader is created and used to read the data. In each iteration of the loop, the `insert_one()` function of the `collection` object is used to write the next row to a document in the collection:

```
....
collection = db["records2"]

## read data line by line and
## insert each row as a document
## into the database collection
fin = open("data/fake_weather_data.csv","r",newline="")
reader = csv.DictReader(fin)
for row in reader:
    collection.insert_one(row)

fin.close()
```

Running `process_large_data.py` should now have the same effect as the `mongoimport` command did before. Processing the data in Python gives you more control over the control over the data import process. For example, it is now possible to modify the code so that the `is_sunny` and `is_cloudy` values are changed to logical before the data is placed in the database.

Once you are finished, you can delete the database by running the following in a mongo shell:

```
> use weather
> db.records2.remove({})
```

For further reading on MongoDB, databases, and working with large data files, you can refer to the *Links and Further Reading* document in the external resources at `https://goo.gl/8S58ra`.

# Summary

In summary, as datasets become larger and larger, it becomes important to consider how to manage memory while processing data, and how to store data to make it easy to work with and retrieve. Sufficiently large datasets should be processed entry by entry and not as a whole in order to preserve memory. For datasets that will need to be accessed frequently, it can be helpful to store and retrieve the data through a local database instance. This concludes the third and final section of *Practical Data Wrangling*! Congratulations!

In this book, I've made an effort to cover a wide range of approaches to data wrangling in order to give you the flexibility to tackle both standard and non-standard data wrangling challenges practically, efficiently, effectively, and with confidence. You should now have a broad and powerful set of tools that you can use to manipulate data and get the results that you need.

Of course, not everything could fit in this book. As you approach various datasets in your work, you will certainly come across challenges that will go beyond the demonstrations used in the chapters of this book, and you will continue to learn new tools and approaches to meet those challenges. As you continue to learn, my hope is that this book will have provided you with a strong starting place, and I hope that you've come away with a new sense of your ability to tackle data wrangling challenges. :)

# Index